We despaired even of Life

As told by the persecuted Believers in
Russia in the early 1900s

E.O.P.Mutton
with
W.S.Chellberg
2023

The quotations from the Bible are generally from the King James Version of the Bible.

Much of the material was supplied by Edwin O.P.Mutton [Read the Preface] grandson of Paul and Erna Cooper. New material (2023) is supplied by Yuri Bakhvarov the great grandson of Daniel Otsing.

The chapter "Forgive me, Natasha" is an excerpt of the autobiography of Sergei Kourdakov after coming to Canada and the USA. Published by Marshall, Morgan & Scott, London UK.

Editing and layout by W.S.Chellberg, June 2020
Revision 1: Feb. 2023

Published by

Saville Street Distribution

Witney, Oxfordshire, England

savstdist@gmail.com

ISBN: 978-0-912868-26-4

Printed and bound by

LuLu Press

www.lulu.com

2023

TABLE of CONTENTS

Map
Preface
Introductory and Important 7
"Forgive Me, Natasha" 9
Group of Brethren Photo 15
Mr. & Mrs. Otsing 16
Biography of Daniel Otsing 17
Otsing Family Photo 1899 18
Early Letters – 1922-1930 19
Begin Letters 21
Explantion – JHL 32
Account of Brethren in Moscow – 1930 33
Letters 1934-1936 – Intro 37
Daniel Otsing's Hymn 52
Last Contact with Daniel Otsing 54

Commentaries Chapter
    Bernt Lindberg 58
    Arne Lidbeck 62
    Remembered in 1997 66

Last Letters – 1968 – 1975 69
Miss Tatjana Stenbock's Conversion 73
Letter Concerning Miss Stenbock 81

THE GENERATION OF FAITH - *1911*
Four Reading Meetings in St. Petersburg

    The Faith Once Delivered... 83
    On Christian Marriage 89
    Preparation of the Heart for the Assembly .. 92
    Christ Continued in His Body of the Earth .. 95

Some Notes on Surrounding Countries

    Poland 100
    Norway & Sweden 104
    Estonia, Latvia, Lithuania 105

The word of God is not bound 106

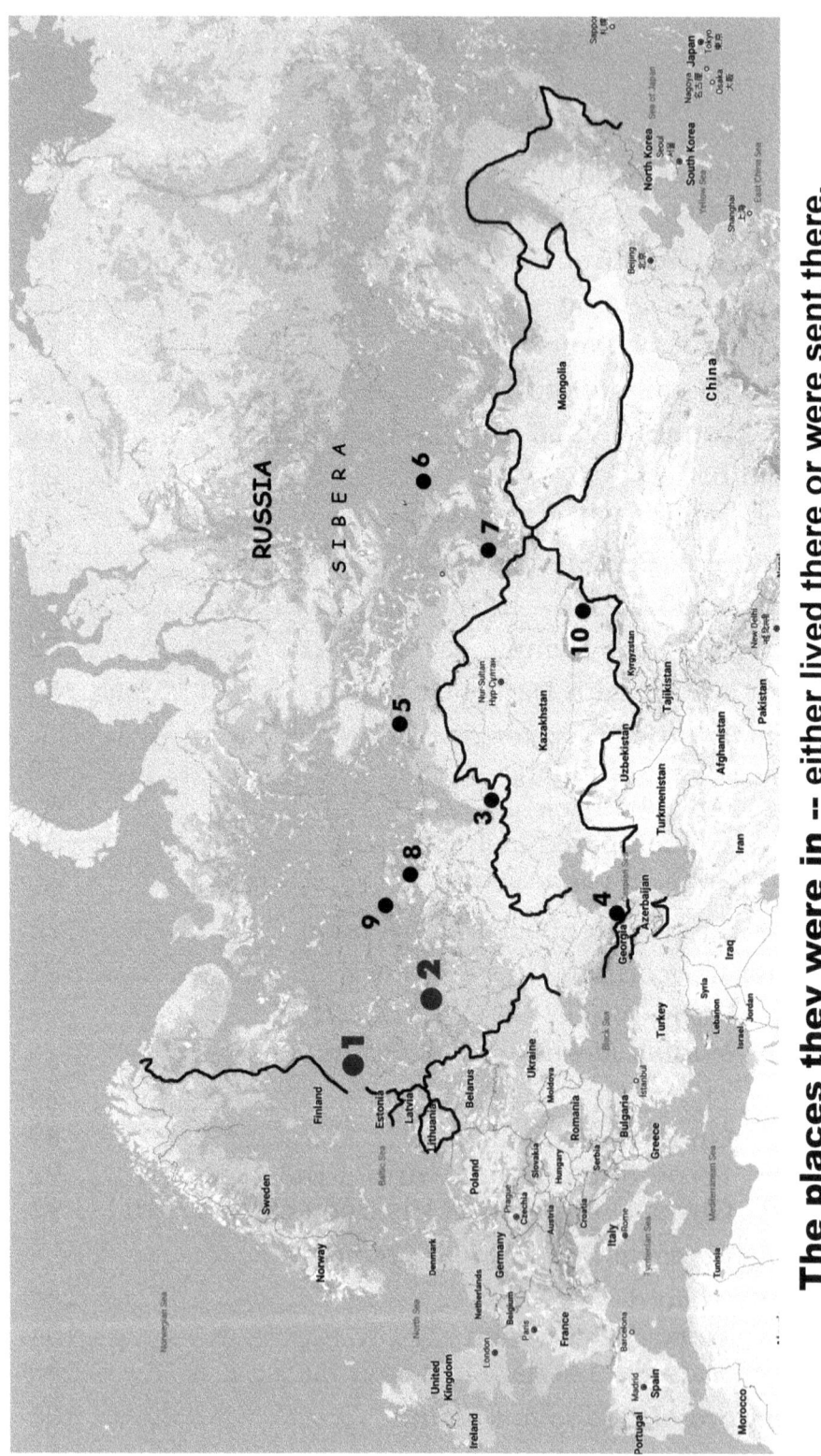

The places they were in -- either lived there or were sent there.

MAP LOCATIONS

1.) Saint Petersburgh before 1914
    Petrograd -- 1914 to 1924
    Leningrad -- 1924 to 1991
    St. Petersburg -- 1991 to current

2.) Moscow
3.) Karangddda, Siberia
4.) Caucasus Mountain area
5.) Tyumen Province
6.) Krasnoyarsk, Siberia
7.) Biysk, Siberia
8.) Wjatka (Vyatka) Province, could not locat Slobodokaja
9.) Kirov, Siberia
10.) Alma Ata, Kzakhstan

The distances in a straight line (which it never was) between some of these places are:

Moscow to St. Petersburg -- 575 miles
Moscow to Alma Ata, Kzakhstan -- 2200 miles
Moscow to Krasnoyarsk, Siberia -- 2900 miles
(measurements are approximate)

PREFACE

My mother and grandparents, among other relatives, were all part of the little company pictured on page 15 of this book. From them I heard of the unbelievable horrors and privations of their lives during the Russian Revolution of 1916 and their subsequent escape to Sweden. I still have the letter sent by that small company commending my grandparents and family to their brethren in Sweden. They also told of the sufferings of those they left behind and who were banished to Siberia. They spoke of eating rats and nettles to stay alive, of guns held to their heads and of fleeing across frozen lakes to freedom.

But above all, they told of piety, simple faith in the Lord Jesus, of clinging to the hope of the church so beautifully expressed in the hymn on page 50, written at the height of the fighting. This hymn enshrines for me the triumph of the faith that pervades this book. It shows how the reality of faith can and has flourished through the darkest times. A coming day will display heaven's delight and appreciation of such spiritual formation; may we who remain be worthy by our lives of such a heritage.

Edwin Mutton
May 2020

This chapter is INTRODUCTORY and IMPORTANT that you read this first.

This book is a collection of correspondence with brethren in Russia in the early years of the Twenteth Century. They describe a few of the hardships the believers there endured. A number of these letters were written to Mr. Paul Cooper who lived with his wife and family in St. Petersburg until the Bolshevik revolution and then was forced to leave. (His wife being a niece of Daniel Otsing's wife.) He, of course, knew the brethren there very well. Several brothers from countries outside Russia visited them and some of these wrote "newsletters" (as I will call them) to alert believers generally as to conditions there. In writing these "newsletters" the writers were able to say what conditions they found, while letters from Russia could not contain certain information due to the government censoring. As one brother notes, some of the brethren used Scripture references to show the real conditions. This is the first publication of these letters.

The next chapter is a portion of the autobiography of a young Russian KGB police officer who was in command of a group whose main occupation was to break up Believer's meetings, and they did it well – and were commended by their superiors. By killing, maiming, and injuring they thought they would 'teach the believers a lesson'. What he came to learn later was that the believers they attacked had something far greater than he had, or any of the police. He began to realize that they were dealing with 'something' far greater than just some poor people. The turning point for him was when he raised his club to strike an old woman who was praying, he suddenly realized she was praying for him, but he started to strike her and someone grabbed hold of his wrist, and when he turned to see who it was there was no one there or nearby. He turned and left the house and ran into the woods totally stunned – and his wrist still hurt. He eventually came to acknowledge that there is a God and he gave his life to

Jesus Christ. At twenty years old he defected to Canada and then the United States (a story in itself) and having become so solidly converted he never tired of speaking of Jesus. The KGB caught up with him in California and he was shot, but not before he wrote his story titled *"Forgive Me, Natasha."* While his story is about the 1960s, it had all started with the Bolshevik revolution in 1917.

I hope I have given you a bit of background of what you are about to read in this book. I, also, hope you will be able to understand that because of censorship most of the letter writers could not speak directly about happenings, persons, and places, so you can imagine what anxiety, heartache, and suffering they had. For example; one young family was torn apart for no reason and the husband sent to hard labor (his wife and little child left to fend for themselves), or another old man hauled into the police station for questioning because of being reported by a KGB spy, then thrown into jail for months. Most of the time it was just because of their belief, but some other reason would be stated. In one case, at least, they were heard singing! They did not dare to mention any of these things in writing. Daniel Otsing, at 85 years old was shipped off to a place in far off Kazakhstan to hard labor of which he shortly died. This happened to almost all that we knew at one time or another. So, as you read this next chapter you may understand.

There are a few things said about Poland, Norway, and Sweden, but not nearly the same persecution. Also, some information about an Estonian sister who was converted in Russia and ended up living in a displaced persons camp near Hamburg, Germany.

It should strengthen our faith and resolve to increase in our testimony and witness of our wonderful Savior, and the God Who can be trusted to do the best for us. One thing that shines out in these letters is how accepting they were in calamity. Much of this information and the letters are supplied by Paul Cooper's grandson, whom we all know as Edwin Mutton.

W.S.Chellberg
April, 2020

A Story of Persecution of Believers in Russia

(Sergei Kourdakov had worked his way up to leadership in a K.G.B. Police unit and part of his work was to stop Believer's meeting together. **This is his account of what they did.***)*

"Nothing in the house – people or furniture – escaped our wrath. We smashed everything in sight. Whoever had turned his house into a secret church building would learn he couldn't do it without losing everything he had. In minutes the house was a shambles--broken tables, chairs, dishes, everything, smashed and scattered all over the room. Half-covered by the debris were the Believers, some unconscious and the rest in agonizing pain.

I saw Victor Matvyev reach and grab for a young girl who was trying to escape to another room. She was a beautiful young girl. What a waste to be a Believer, I thought. Victor caught her, picked her up, lifted her above his head and held her high in the air for a second. She was pleading, "Don't, please don't. Dear God, help us!" Victor threw her so hard she hit the wall at the same height she was thrown, then dropped to the floor, semi-conscious, moaning. Victor turned and laughed and exclaimed, "I'll bet the idea of God went flying out of her head." But I was thinking, She's a really beautiful girl. I wished I had met her under better circumstances.

"Get the books," I shouted. We scoured the room, looking for Bibles and any torn-up literature they might have. I grabbed a hand-written child's exercise book with scribbled Bible verses from the hands of an old woman. She was partly conscious and kept moaning, "Why? Why?" It wasn't so much a question, but an outcry of agony, coming from deep within her soul. "Why?"

"Get those two men!" I ordered, pointing to the two leaders who matched the description Nikiforov had given me. "Get them out to the truck." And while a couple of my men moved to obey, the rest of us went around the room taking identification papers from the Believers and noting them. I got the beautiful girl's identification card. I had a special interest in her. Her name was Natasha Zhdanova. After getting their names, we could find them any time we wanted.

The job was done. It was time to go. I ordered my men out... We had done our work well.

On the way back to the police station, I began questioning the two men we had arrested. But first they had a question for us. "How did you know ?"

"Well, what do you think, you stupid fools? We have our people, our spies. You're the easiest people in the world to find." They didn't seem surprised. "You invite people to come to your secret churches, don't you?" I continued. "If you don't want to be found, why do you do that?"

"You don't understand," the underground pastor said. "We know there are spies. We're not that foolish. But we have a great responsibility to invite people to come to God. How could we invite people to God and spread our faith and keep outsiders away? We know, of course, when we talk to people about God, some will be spies. We know the risk." He paused for a moment, and I thought he was through, but soon he began again. "But we feel that our responsibility to share with others is more important than our own safety."

What stupid fools, I thought. How could our country be endangered .by people like that?

...Three days later eight members of my operations group and I were sitting around the waiting room, on duty in case there should be any calls. We did this stand-by duty once or twice a week. At about 7 p.m. Nikiforov's phone rang and seconds later he came hurrying out of his office, shouting, "Kourdakov, Konrdakov, get your men ready and take off right now!"

"Where do we go ?" I asked, smelling action.

"Nagornaya Street." And he gave the house number. Either somebody had noticed something suspicious at that address or one of the spies had found the meeting in progress and reported it. At any rate, it was going on right now!

I hurried my men out to the truck, then ordered Victor to drive off at high speed. Either Victor was the world's worst driver, taking. so many unnecessary risks, or he was the world's best driver, proving it by his uncanny ability to miss all the traffic on the road by the smallest margin.

"Cut the siren," I shouted, as we neared the target area. We roared up Nagornaya Street, jumped out before the truck stopped rolling and rushed to the front of the house, crashing through the door. To our astonishment, they were all young people. Not a grey head there! We had found a secret young people's meeting in progress, catching them completely by surprise. We went right to work on them, grabbing them and swinging them about, slapping and shoving them.

"That's him. Grab him," I said, pointing to the twenty-three year-old youth who was their leader. Some of our guys rushed him and began knocking him around. Some of my men were punching the others around, using them playfully as punching bags. I quickly surveyed the room and saw a sight I couldn't believe! There she was, that same girl! It couldn't be. But it was. Only three nights before, she had been at the other meeting and had been viciously thrown across the room. It was the first time I really got a good look at her. She was more beautiful than I had first remembered, with long, flowing blonde hair, large blue eyes and smooth skin – one of the most naturally beautiful girls I ever have seen.

Victor saw her too and shouted, "She's back! Look, guys, she's back again!" . –

"Well," I shouted, "it doesn't look like you did such a great job, the last time, Victor. You failed to teach her a lesson. Now it's my turn!"

I picked her up and flung her on a table face down. Two of us stripped her clothes off. One of my men held her down and I began to beat her with my open hand as hard as I could, hitting her again and again. My hands began to sting under the blows. Her skin started to blister. I continued to beat her, until pieces of bloody flesh came off on my hand. She moaned but fought desperately not to cry. To suppress her cries, she bit her lower lip until it was bitten through and blood ran down her chin.

At last she gave in and began sobbing. When I was so exhausted I couldn't raise my arm for even one more blow, and her backside was a mass of raw flesh, I pushed her off the table, and she collapsed on the floor.

Leaving her, I looked around, almost exhausted, to see how the rest of our group was doing. The young Believers were lying around the wrecked room. There was no point in prolonging the job so, knowing we already had the leader, I shouted, "We've got our man! Get the names of those people now and let's get out of here."

When we arrived back at the police station, there stood Nikiforov standing at the door greeting us with a smile. "Well, my children," he said, "I see that was quick work."

"Here's your man," I said, shoving the leader of the group at Nikiforov, who had him taken downstairs immediately for "interrogation". I began to look over the names of the other young people who were caught in the meeting. I could understand foolish old people who were infected with religion before Communism. But young people believing in God! It was just too much for me to grasp. These were people my age, my generation. It baffled me.

But that one girl had certainly been taught a lesson. I chided Victor once more. "You just didn't have it, old boy," I said. "But I took care of her tonight. We'll never see Gorgeous again."

The next day...

When all was ready, we burst in, swinging clubs wildly. The shocked, bewildered Believers began to scatter, trying to protect themselves from the rain of blows. The meeting room was small, and with eight Believers and six of us it was crowded. There was lots of noise – shouts and screams.

This isn't going to take long, I thought. And then I caught a glimpse of a familiar face. I couldn't believe it! There she was again – Natasha. Zhdanova!

As several of my men saw her too. Alex Gulyaev moved toward Natasha, hatred filling his face, his club raised high above his head.

Then something I never expected to see suddenly happened. Without warning, Victor jumped between Natasha and Alex, facing Alex head on.

"Get out of my way," Alex shouted angrily.

Victor's feet didn't move. He raised his club and said menacingly, "Alex, I'm telling you, don't touch her! No one touches her!"

I listened in amazement. Incredibly, Victor, one of my most brutal men, was protecting one of the Believers! "Get back!" he shouted to Alex. "Get back or I'll let you have it." He shielded Natasha, who was cowering on the floor.

Angered, Alex shouted, "You want her for yourself, don't you!"

"No," Victor shouted back. "She has something we don't have! Nobody touches her! Nobody!"

I had to break this up, and fast. Alex's violent temper would mean a fight. "Look, Alex," I shouted, pointing to another Believer trying to get away. "Get him!" Distracted, Alex took out after him. I breathed a sigh of relief.

Victor still stood with his arms out, protecting Natasha, daring Alex or anyone to take a step toward her. Natasha stood behind Victor, not understanding what was happening. This was not the kind of treatment she had come to expect from this group. I nodded to her, then motioned for her to get out. She turned and hurried out. I nodded a sign of approval.

For one of the few times in my life, I was deeply moved. It was like the time when my friend Sasha died back at Barysevo. Natasha did have something! She had been beaten horribly. She had been warned and threatened. She had gone through unbelievable suffering, but here she was again. Even though

Victor had been moved and recognized it. She had something we didn't have. I wanted to run after her and ask, "What is it?" I wanted to talk to her, but she was gone. This heroic Christian girl who had suffered so much at our hands somehow both touched and troubled me very much.

Shortly afterwards Natasha left Kamchatka and returned to her home in the Ukraine. The ridicule and mockery from her co-workers at the newspaper [where she worked as a proofreader] made life all but unbearable for her.

...Natasha had shaken all my notions about Believers."

He ends his book with this... "And I have in my heart a message I want to pass to those Believers in Russia who have helped so much to change my life. I put this message in this book, hoping that in some way, at some time, it can reach them and they will understand.

To Mrs. Litovchenko, the paralysed wife of the pastor whom we killed that Sunday afternoon along the Elizovo River: I wish to tell you that I am sorry, more than you can ever know.

To Nina Rudenko, the beautiful little teenage girl whose life was ruined by my attack group, I ask, "Please forgive us."

And, finally, to Natasha, whom I beat terribly and who was willing to be beaten a third time for her faith, I want to say, "Natasha, largely because of you, my life is now changed and I am a fellow Believer in Christ with you. I have a new life before me."

God has forgiven me; I hope you can also. Thank you, Natasha, wherever you are. I will never, never forget you!"

On January 1, 1973 he was apparently assassinated by the KGB in a motel room in California for his speaking out about the persecution of believers by the KGB in Russia. They had warned him when he lived in Toronto. The above story is in his own words and occurred in the 1960s.

From the book – "Forgive Me, Natasha" by Sergei Kourdakov (1951-1973)

* * * * *

Brethren in Leningrad 1913

1. J.H.Lewis - England
2. Mrs. Magalene Muhs
3. Mrs. Jenny Otsing
4. Mrs. Kilgast
5. Mrs. Emma Fehst
6. Miss Bergman
7. Miss Vera Schmidt
8. Mrs. Erna Cooper - Sweden
9. Felix Fehst - Estonia
10. Wassily Otsing
11. Paul Cooper
12. Mrs. Katarine Cooper
13. Daniel Otsing
14. Mrs. Schmidt
15. Mrs. Wilhelmina Otsing
16. Michael Muhs
17. Miss Helene Cooper (Lena)
18. Miss Sofie Cooper
19. Mr. Adolf Otsing

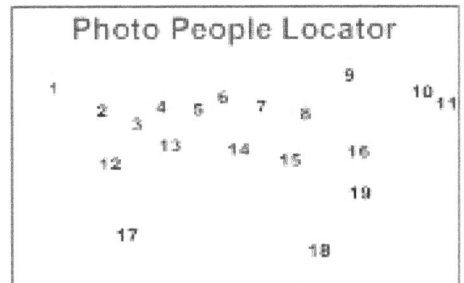

Mr. Daniel and Mrs. Otsing
(Daniel 1850 to 1937)

"Be thou faithful unto death, and I will give to thee the crown of life." (Revelation 2: 10)

Biography of Daniel Otsing

Daniel was *born* on the 17th July 1854 at Leevaku, Ruusa, Toolamaa, Rapina Parish, Polva County Estonia. He was one of five children.

Daniel was *married* on the 17th May 1877 in Neuhausen, Enz in Baden-Württemberg, Germany, to Wilhelmine Albertina Auguste Habeck
Children:
    Hugo Alfons Hans   1878-1938
    Selma Johanna 1879-?
    Alma 1881-1953
    Adolph Aleksander 1889-1976
    Wassily Friedrich Otsing 1885-1938
    Alexander Eduard 1883-1960

Daniel and family moved to St. Petersburg sometime before 1899. He, and some of his family came amongst the little company of believers in that city.

Wassily, his son, married Jenni Nystrom, a sister of my Grandmother, Erna Cooper and he signed a letter of commendation when my Grandparents Cooper and family moved to Stockholm in 1922. (I still have the original.)

Daniel was arrested on 21st April 1935 (81 years old) for "counter revolutionary sectarian activity". His wife had died earlier that year. He was exiled, now over 81, for three years to Kazakhstan, where he lived in the village of Leninskoye. *He was re-arrested on 3rd November 1937 and sentenced to execution.* This was carried out, probably by firing squad, on 29th November 1937. Daniel is buried in Tallina Siselinna Kalmistu, 3 Staadioni, Tallinn, Tallinna Iinn, Harju County, Estonia. The date of death on his tombstone is 15th January 1939 which may indicate a delay in returning his body to Estonia.

(Information from Yuri Bakhvarov in Archangelsk, Russia. He is a great-grandson of Daniel Otsing and has the family papers.)

Otsing Family about 1899

Top L. to R.:
Alma, Hugo A. Hans, Selma Johanna, Alexander Eduard
Seated L. to R.:
Wassily Friedrich, (Mrs.) Wilhelmine Albertine, Daniel, Adolph Alexander.

The Early Letters

1922 to 1930

TRANSLATION OF A LETTER FROM A BROTHER IN MOSCOW TO MR HAROLD PETTER, MONKSEATON

Moscow, 10 March 1922

Dear Brother in the Lord,

I am greatly surprised by this, that the brethren in England are writing to me, a place where I personally have no one I know, yet still I receive not only a letter but also a parcel. Vcrily the ways of the Lord are wonderful!

By the blood of Christ we are put together into one and therefore there must be with us one heart and the same thoughts and those feelings which are in Christ Jesus (Philippians 2:5).

Beloved brethren, you have practically expressed brotherly love (Hebrews 13:1). It is not given to us to know one another according to flesh (2 Corinthians 5:16). However, the Holy Spirit through the work which is accomplished by the Lord unites us from all tribes and peoples and languages into one complete all — that is, the Church, the body of Christ: "the mystery which was hidden from eternal days and generations" (Colossians 1:26).

How we would desire to speak with you, even by letter, in your English language. It is true that at the present time for me it is impossible, but the Lord has foreseen this and has made it possible for you, beloved brother, to express yourself in Russian. May the Most High have honour and glory and thanksgiving.

The parcel, which was addressed by brother Lewis to Moscow I received through the American Relief Commission in Moscow on 18 February this year. Before I received your letter from England through brother Fehst, I was thinking that the parcel was addressed to me from brother Paul Cooper, who is the only brother who is now abroad. It is evident that according to human reasoning, to receive parcels from brothers about whom one has only heard was a real wonder. But it is a fact. For all this we have brought our thanksgiving to the Lord who teaches us to care not for ourselves but for others (Philippians 2:4; 2 Corinthians 9:10-15).

In regard to any hindrance from the Soviet Government, the parcels are received through the American Relief Committee. There need be no fear about it. The Soviet Government does not interfere with these matters.

From believers in Moscow we are only one family left, but in spite of all we believe that the Lord has here His men who have not bowed the knee to Baal (1 Kings 19:18). We have been thinking that in Moscow the same thing would be repeated which was already with brother Daniel Petersson-Otsing, who lived at one time alone in the town of Slobodskoj in the district of Wjatka. Afterwards, it has pleased the Lord to have there also brother Julius Kraft from Petrograd, but now there are at the feet of Christ several other souls.

As a conclusion to my letter I want once more to express in this letter my joy that surrounded me when seeing the substantiation of brotherly love, by brethren who are separated from us by such great distances: Russia — England. Nevertheless the love of Christ unites our hearts together into one. Glory, glory, honour and thanksgiving to the Lord Jesus Christ. "Peace to the brethren and love with faith from God the Father and the Lord Jesus Christ. Grace with all them that love the Lord Jesus Christ in incorruption. Amen." (Ephesians 6:23-24).

Greetings from us in Moscow to the Lord's Assembly in England.

Your brother in the Lord

Alexander Sajonchkowsky

TRANSLATION OF A LETTER FROM DANIEL OTSING TO MR JH PENSON

19 November 1924

My very dear Ivan Alexseyevich,

I was delighted to receive your letter of 10 October 1924; do forgive me for taking so long to reply. Time flies very fast and my energy and memory are so poor that in my daily activities I fail to get everything done that I would like to. But how wonderful it is for us to look upon the glorified Christ in heaven Who comforts us in our earthly difficulties, saying: "sufficient for thee is my grace, for my strength is made perfect in weakness." 2 Corinthians 12:9.

The Lord gave me the opportunity to visit our brother Aleksandr Yulianovich and I spent 16 days at his place. The Lord wonderfully blessed us for those days. At our brother's request we considered, among other things, the book of the prophet Daniel and we saw in him (Daniel):

1 A wonderful prototype for Christ; how much love of Christ and how many thoughts of God were in his heart, when God called His people "thy people"! This trait of Christ was shared most of all by Moses, the apostle Paul and others;

2 We saw in him the prototype of the gathering (the Church) in witness in the midst of Babylon, i.e. amidst the collapse of the church today;

3 We saw that all world events with peoples are related to the pasturing of the pious remnant and to the revealing of the glory of Christ; we also saw in what conditions the Lord will give His revelations to his bondmen in the last days of the present age.

We take it in turns to visit our brother A. Yu. so that the breaking of bread may continue without interruption. Sister Yelena Pavlovna will go there now, until the Lord provides another and a third witness in that place.

We very often remember you with love and joy in the Lord. I send you from myself, my wife and from all the other brothers and sisters much love and to all the pious near you.

Daniel Petrovich (Daniel Otsing)

COPY OF A LETTER FROM DANIEL OTSING

Leningrad 5 October 1926

My beloved brother in the Lord,

I ought to have written to you a long time ago — please excuse me. I desired first to see if I could visit the brethren in Wjatka or not. Now, thanks be to God, the journey is already behind me. I have just returned and am able to give you an account of my visit.

"The Lord giveth power to the faint; and to him that hath no might he increaseth strength"; so He was with us even in the past summer. He allowed us to hire by the love of the brethren a little summer cottage with two rooms, not far from Leningrad, where the feeblest sisters could one after another strengthen their bodies in the fresh air during the summertime. Also, in our neighborhood Alexander Julianowitsch from Moscow placed his family for the summer. We could have readings together looking through the whole of Exodus. Through these readings, the Lord has opened the truth to the teacher of Brother Z's children. She was one of the Evangelical Christians, but now she has come to love the truth. The short visit of brother Iwan Alexejewitsch has been to us a blessed help and a spiritual encouragement. We cannot sufficiently thank the God and Father of our Lord Jesus Christ for the gift of love from the saints which came to us through your hand. How wonderful! Already after two months staying here I was strengthened in body and spirit so that I could start my journey to the brethren at Wjatka with joy and delight.

The Lord gave to our brother Fedor Iwanowitsch a little holiday and we both started our happy journey on 12 September. The only grief I had was that I could not find on earth my beloved brother Rodd whom I expected to see, as the Lord had taken him home to Himself in the glory. The Lord has made it unexpectedly better than we could hope as it is very much better to be with Christ. Now it remains to us to have delight in that in which Christ has delight "To the saints that are on the earth, and to the excellent — in them is all my delight" Psalm 16:3.

After two days journey of about 1200 km we stopped to visit the nearest brother who lived about 22 km from the railway. We were able to reach him only after 6 hours traveling with much trouble, as the way was so bad and it was a dark night and raining. The brethren received us with great joy; they are scattered, about 10 to 30 km from one another. To bring them together for a special reading of the Word of God, brother K. had at once to send his son as a messenger to the next brother; and that one sent to the next one, and so on. In that way the brethren came together the next evening and we could be strengthened and happy sitting at the feet of our Lord and Saviour Jesus.

After four days my brother Fedor Iwanowitsch had to return, as his holidays came to an end. The Lord has given me grace and strength to remain two weeks among the brethren. The readings on weekdays have been more of a private character because of the long distances between the brethren. On the Lord's Day there is breaking of bread in three or four places, each one with his next brother. The afternoon of this day is used to be together with all the brethren who are invited as guests for that purpose (2 (Corinthians 8:13). They come together with their wives and children and so the Word is read for the edification of the saints. I was present on such an occasion. I have seen the brethren with their wives and children. Among the wives have been some who are not yet in fellowship. The Lord gave us to read 1 Corinthians 10. The cardinal point was the people of God baptized in the cloud and in the sea, journeying through the wilderness of this world to the glory under the leadership of Christ and His Spirit. We touched also the thought about the home-priesthood of each brother according to Exodus 12 etc. On the next Lord's Day afternoon we read Exodus 21 – Christ as the true Servant and the heavenly Head, now of His heavenly bride in heavenly places (Ephesians 1 and 5) as also in a coming day for the new Jerusalem. He is the same for His earthly bride on mount Zion (Revelation 14) of which we have much to learn now.

The Lord has blessed us with His Spirit's quiet movements. In all, I have had great comfort with the brethren, my heart is refreshed with joy and thanks to God about the good spiritual condition of the brethren and I pray to God that they may be more abundant in faith and love which are in Christ Jesus. At the same time I pray that the Lord may give two things to the brethren. First, that they may have understanding that God desires to bring His worshippers and priests afier the end of the thanksgiving in a special way near to the holy place according to Leviticus 8:31; 10:12-14; 1 Corinthians 14:26. And second, to maintain the testimony of the assembly outwardly (Ephesians 6:15; Revelation 22:17). I have confidence in the Lord that if somebody is otherwise minded, this also God shall reveal unto them (Philippians 3:15).

Also, the great enemy of souls did not neglect to cause here and there somebody to consider the flesh and to trust to the flesh to bring the assembly away from simplicity as to the Christ, but the Lord has wonderfully kept the brethren. We see in this God's answer to the prayers of the saints, the precious fruit of the blessed service of the faithful High Priest before God in heaven — what a comfort to us.

With this precious comfort I took farewell of the brethren, who expressed their hope soon to meet one another again. Brother K. accompanied me on the railway to Wajtka, where a brother G. lives with his mother. He went a year ago to the Evangelical Christians together with brother J ., but soon he saw his fault and recognized and confessed it. At the same time he left the Evangelicals. Since then he has stood alone with his mother without fellowship, but now it seems that the brother G. (son and mother) are fully restored by the Lord Himself. They have waited a year, after they left unrighteousness, for fellowship with our brethren. Now our brother K., who came with me to Wjatka, could take this good news to our brethren. We stayed two days with our brother G. Brother K went back to our brethren and I went to Leningrad. Praise be to the Lord that He was with us with His Spirit at Wjatka. Even brother J., who is still with the Evangelicals, sent his greetings to me before I left with the expression of his sorrow that he couldn't see me. I sent him my love and said that I should be glad to help him on my next visit if the Lord will. It seems that the Lord is speaking to him.

The apartments of the brethren are only of one room without water closet [toilet] and are not suitable for a traveling brother to stay in. Only two brethren have a house of two rooms; to those I went. Only one brother was living near a post-connection. The lodging of brother G at Wjatka is only one room. The God and Father of our Lord Jesus Christ be praised for all His grace and mercy in His Son our Lord, in whom He blessed us on this journey. He alone can make it possible if it pleases Him that we can visit our beloved brethren in Siberia the next time, but they are twice as far away as the brethren in Wjatka, of whom one brother, Egor Wassiljewitsch, will soon write to you. Please give our love to all the saints who are with you, through the grace of our Lord Jesus Christ and the love of God and the fellowship of the Holy Spirit, fellow-workers of our joy.

Your brother in the Lord,

Daniel Otsing

COPY OF A FROM DANIEL OTSING TO PAUL COOPER

Pavel Pavelowitsch (Paul Cooper)   Leningrad, 6 October 1926

Beloved brother in the Lord,

It is a long time since I had a letter from you. I believe you must be very busy. Brother Iwan Alexejewitsch, who visited us last summer, told us a bit about you. I hope that both yourself and your dear ones are well. Now I should like to ask you again, my dear brother, to translate the enclosed letter and send it to brother Lewis. Greet your dear wife and children from my wife, Jenny and Wassili. We are reasonably well, except for frailty and oflentimes ailing in body, but it is precious to be led towards glory by the Good Shepherd.

Your brother in the Lord,
D Otsing

TRANSLATION OF A LETTER TO P. COOPER

My dear Brother,   Leningrad, Feb. 21, 1928

I have just received the gift of love sent for the needy brethren, widows and aged ones. Thank God for His great love, which binds His saints together. It is the bond of perfectness. I recently received news from the Brethren in Siberia and Wjalka. They are growing spiritually in the Lord. There are individual cases of trials, for which we are waiting before the Lord in much prayer. it is precious for us to see how God is training His own. If we are so much attached to the earth, He has ways and means of releasing us, so that we might seek that which is above.

According to the daily journals 10,000 Mennonites are emigrating from the south, to Canada. and South America. These. are believers, but far the main part earthly minded Christiana. The Lord has used many in their midst as Evangelists. All nations are the subjects of His grace and mercy, and He causes the gospel of His Son to be proclaimed to them. How wrongly men act, in denying this gracious God, the One who desires to have them as His sons and daughters. All this leads us again and again to persistent prayer for His work and for all men. Greetings in the Lord to you all, also brother Lewis.

Your affectionate brother,

D. Otsing

NOTE: I hold official receipts signed by the Brethren in the different places, acknowledging Bibles to the amount of 140. J.H.Lewis

---

TRANSLATION OF A LETTER FROM MISS M.

My Dear E,   Leningrad, March 22, 1928

It is a long time since I wrote to you. L received your letter, but not the calendar. I am sorry for this, but if the Lord permitted it, we accept this from His hand. Yes, we are under pressure from all side, but the Lard is faithful, and His love endless and unchangeable. If we had not the Word of God, we might many times despair. This winter has been poorer in spiritual ministry than the previous one. Our circle is becoming narrower, soon it will be literally two or three. The spiritual condition of each individual is known to Himself, but He will not give up one, because he is purchased at such great cost. I grieve to tell that three brothers have left us. It is sorrowful, as we are so few already. We so need more brothers! The last two Lord's Days we four sisters, on our side, had no brother, so could not break bread. Our dear Lord knows it. Our brother F has had to leave the city on account of unemployment, but we hear that he has another post in prospect. We shall see how the Lord will lead him. You will grieve to hear that our dear Brother Pawloff's daughter fell into the well and was drowned. She had gone in the evening to fetch water, and probably slipped, and fell in. She was a child of God, so the dear Lord took her home. It was a powerful sermon for those left behind. Thus He speaks to His own. Mrs. M sends love.

We live near each other, but are scarce able to see each other save an Lord's day. For a time we went to her house on Fridays, but this has had to cease. His name be praised for everything. It all comes from strong, eternal, Divine love. Glory be to Him forever. Goodbye dear E.

Yours affectionately in Christ,

A. M.

TRANSLATION OF PART OF A LETTER

My Very Beloved Erna,   Moscow, March 22, 1928

Oh, how I rejoiced in your letter, and the little passport photo. Tears came into my eyes, and with them, an intense longing to see your face. How necessary for a Christian to have exercise and experience in this life, because it brings profit and blessing. Dearest Erna recently I have gone through many testings but cannot speak to you about them. All we can do is to pray for one another. Only the Lord knows, how He will lead each one of us, and which way. Your remark about Elijah in 1 Chronicles, has cheered me. I knew that all we pass through, is for the blessing of our spiritual being, and the glorifying of His name. The Psalmist says in Psalm 119:71, "It is good for me that I have been afflicted; that I might learn Thy statutes." How sorry I am that you are moving further away from us, but I am glad far your sakes. I do not give up hopes yet of seeing you again, if the Lord will. Dearest Erna, don't be surprised if I don't write. In spirit I am always with yuu. I hope to spend our summer holidays with our dear brother Otsing. May the Lord preserve him to us. He is advanced in years, though so capable. I love a talk with him.

Our heartfelt greetings in the Lord's love.

Z. Marussja

NOTE: Our dear sister's husband is in prison, The saints might read between the lines as to conditions there. We do not knew yet if our brother is released. They are afraid in mention it. J. H. L.

EXTRACT OF A LETTER

Dear E,   Leningrad, March 22, 1928

Perhaps you will write and send us the addresses of the Brethren in Germany. We should so like to have Revelation and Laviticus by C.A.C. We have Genesis and Exodus. We are now few here. We come together an Mondays at 9 p.m. for prayer. First we read a little and then we pray. Ah! we have so much to pray about. We have watched and prayed too little, hence the enemy has succeeded in getting in amongst us. But the Lord is great in His goodness towards us. We should like to have some books in German, but they can only be obtained through private persons. Pray for us.

Yours in His love,

A.M.

NOTE: I have recently heard from our Brother Ruckbrodt in Leipzig, saying that he has several times sent books to the Brethren, but they have been returned with "Religious books are forbidden" stamped on the labels. J.H.L.

TRANSLATION OF A LETTER TO J.H.LEWIS

Beloved Brother in the Lord,   Leningrad, April 26, 1928

I am thankful to God that He gives the saints the desire to supply or Brethren here with Bibles, and also to distribute to others, who are spiritually and temporally poor. (Matthew 5:3, James 2:5.) We have received 45 Bibles. and 20 New Testaments. The brethren in Moscow and Pargola have also received their parcels. I am awaiting news from Siberia, but I believe they, and also at Wjatka, have received their allotted parcels. I hope also that they will write you. I pray the Lord to give me, and the Brethren, grace and wisdom in our daily conversation with men that the Biblas sent may go into the hands of those who are thirsty. As to the work of the Lord in general, one can say that there is a noticeable awakening of the masses. In the early part of the past ten years, the

Churches (Orthodox, Protestant, etc.) were not well attended, but now they are crowded. The clergyman make the greatest effort as preach evangelical sermons, because the evangelical movement of believers, and the behavior of the lawless, has driven them to it. As a whole, Christians have begun to feel the chastisement of God. They all receive the testimony sf John the Baptist, "Repent." "Maybe the Lord is preparing the people for the second part of John's testimony, according to John 1: "Beheld the Lamb of God," so as to gather them afterwards to Christ risen. It is a pity that the masses of Christians in our country do not go beyond Golgotha. But the risen and glorified Lord in His personal service, through the Spirit, according to 2 Corinthians 3 desires to lead them into these things. We hear that small groups of believers (not satisfied with the official Service of course) try to edify themselves at home at the feet of Jesus. We are waiting upon the Lord in prayer that He may bring us in touch with such souls.

Our beloved brother F. has had to leave Leningrad on account of the factory closing. He owns a little farm near N. We miss him much, but the Lord will use him there, where there are some believing souls. As we have many sisters here. readings are carried on in many houses. Each group is found together twice a week. Nearly every house is surrounded by infidel neighbors, so we are unable to sing aloud. We pray that the Lord may send us more brothers.

Our dear brother P. comes to Leningrad 3 or 4 times in the week to help the saints. The sisters also, according possibility, come together to pray.

I close now with hearty greetings to you and your wife, and all the saints, from us all here. The widow M. M. sends love. She is weak and suffers with her heart. Pray dear Brethren for the work of the Lord in our land.

Yours knit together in our Lord,

D. Otsing

EXTRACTS OF A LETTER

Leningrad, May 13, 1928

We are hoping to go to Ukrania. Rooms are so much cheaper there, and milk four timers cheaper than in the Leningrad district. Fruit is also plentiful there, and the air fresher. I wanted la take Mrs. Muhs with us, but she is too weak. We have recently been robbed of all our linen. We had but a day before taken same away. In general everything is coming in an end. They have done service 14 years, but now all is in rags. There is a poor dear mother with eight children, who comes at times and reads with me, and get refreshed in spirit. Poor soul. They often go to bed hungry. They have no blankets, but just put their clothes ever them. The children are very pretty, but it is all so painful to see all this and unable to help them. She is a believer, and a dear upright soul.

Affectionately yours,

J.O.

TRANSLATION OF A LETTER TO J.H.LEWIS

My Dear Brother in Christ,   Leningrad, June 12, 1928

Your dear letter of the 26th duly to hand. I thank you for the nice thoughts as to "how various men responded to the love of Christ." How precious to the Lord when we without reserve, surrender ourselves to Himself, for His own sake. "They first gave their own selves to the Lord," 2 Corinthians 8:5. "The love of Christ constrains us," in this we meditated on those precious thoughts, and it was a blessing to us.

I have now had news from Wjatka and Siberia. The Bibles have been receivad by our Brethren. Lately we have been in touch with same other believers who are not organized like the Evangelical Christians, but unfortunately they have made it as a center of all their activities, to obtain the gifts according to 1 Corinthians 12. Many such believers are found among the Finns and Estonians in the country districts around

Leningrad. We would like to be a help to them. I now close with hearty greetings from us all, to the saints generally.

Your brother, who loves you in Christ,

D.Otsing

TRANSLATION OF A LETTER TO J.H.L.

Dear Brother in the Lord,   Bischla, Siberia, July 28, 1928

Your letter of 1926, I am ashamed to say has not been answered. I have had the desire, but could not before now. Through mercy We are preserved. The little company here meet in two places, 4 versts (2.75 miles, or 4.4 kilometers) apart, three brothers and sisters in the village of Chorzovo, and the same in Bischla. One aged brother has just been received into fellowship, from the village of Bischla. There are others who desire, but we are waiting upon the Lord for them. One brother has been among the Pentecostals, but has now left them, and we have had some meetings and readings over the word with him. There are others likewise touched by the truth, about whom I wrote you in a former letter. They come from time to time to the meetings, and it is evident that they receive light, and seek to spread it among the Pentecostals. We partake of the Lord's Supper in the villages mentioned, but come together in one place, once a week, in read the Scriptures. We came together for readings four times during the week. Now my dear brother I must close. Please salute from us all the saints.

Your Brother in the Lord,

J.Zagarskich

EXPLANATION BY J.H.L.

During the past year instruction in the schools and young people's clubs, of hatred to religion, have continued like others since the Second Revolution broke out over the land, has been marked by strong opposition to the religious sphere. Mighty powers have been active, to hinder and work against the gospel. Legislative measures, temporary and changing administrative statutes, stc., circulation of atheistic literature, instruction in the schools and young people's clubs of hatred of religion, continue to be used, as their weapons of war. Sowers of the word, and those who have shown them hospitality and support, have been dragged off to the courts and condemned to imprisonment, fines and persecution. On the other hand, there has been, specially in same provinces, more liberty to preaeh the gospel. The greatest difficulty with these who can preach, is the lack of time and means to enable them to answer the many calls to "come and teach us the way to God." There seems, however, to be a change far the better. Those in position, have publicly acknowledged, that the persecution of religion is a mistake, and suggest other means of attack. It is clearly a camouflage to cover their retreat. Atheism has suffered a defeat in their attack upon the throne of God, and the longing after God in the hearts of the Russian people. The spiritual awakening, which has been going on for some years, continues to spread, though perhaps, with slower movement.

Account of a visit to brethren in Moscow and Leningrad in 1930

The brethren in Moscow walking with us have increased in numbers in recent years. There are now nine breaking bread there and one or two others are interested and come to the meetings. They meet on Lord's Day at the home of our brother and sister K. as they did four years ago. Our brother K. is a great help to the saints there and with it has a very quiet and sweet spirit. The same is to be said about our sister, his wife, and indeed the affection of all the company one to another is very marked.

Our brother Z. has been longest at Moscow of them and was the only brother there when I saw them six years ago. He spent nearly two and a half years in prison and came out in April last. The nature of his offence is not easy to discover. Like many others in Russia who are imprisoned, he knows very little why, it would seem, of the exact grounds of the charge, but in effect it is that he was working for himself and not for the Government. This was not illegal, but lays those who do it open to suspicion. All the brethren in Moscow are now working in the service of the Government in one form or another of its numerous branches. Our sister, Z's his wife, must have suffered much in his absence. She then worked in a factory.

Our brother and sister J. have been in fellowship about a year. He is an intelligent brother of great boldness and faith. Our brother V. has also not been with them very long. He married a couple of years ago our sister H. Cooper, sister of our brother Paul Cooper of Ilford.

Our brethren find the so-called "five day week" very trying. In practice all are called upon to work long hours, and it is only one week in five that their rest day falls on Lord's Day, and it is rare if at all that all are free on Lord's Day.

[FIVE-DAY WEEK NOTE: *In 1929 the Soviets implemented a five-day work week, which meant 5 days after 5 days over and over. Each worker was supposed to be given one day of rest in each 5 days, which was assigned without respect to when family or friends had their day off. What we consider a month consisted of 6 five-day weeks for a total of 30 days, but the worker had only 6 days off in that month, however, time was not counted in months. It made it nearly impossible for brethren to have meetings or the Lord's Supper except in the evening, because they were not usually given time off together, nor was there any day they could call the Lord's Day. This lasted until 1940, hence the comment about the "five-day week".*]

* * * * *

In consequence they have to break bread in the evening. This is followed by a reading, which thus goes on until late at night. They meet also on Thursday for prayer and reading the Scriptures. The brethren are happy together and free in each other's company. The cutting off of material hopes and most material comforts has, under the power of the Spirit, led them to value only that which links them with the Lord and His people. One felt that divine things were all that were left in a very real sense, and that this was felt and realized there.

They were reading Proverbs on Thursday evenings and Romans (chapter 6) on Lord's days. On two occasions we took up John's gospel — on one occasion the fourteenth chapter and, to some extent, the fifteenth — the Spirit as Comforter — and on another occasion the seventeenth chapter — suggested by our brother J. in whose house we met that evening.

The brethren pray and especially ask for the prayers of those in other places, that the Lord's day may be restored to them. They are happy to accept what is granted to them, but it is no doubt difficult to realize the thought of "the first day of the week" in the conditions under which they now have to live and work.

Though cut off from much interchange with brethren elsewhere, those in Moscow and Leningrad feel deeply the spiritual bonds which bind them to the Lord's people throughout the world, especially those with whom they are walking. They repeatedly asked me to convey their thanks and recognition of the prayers of the saints.

Their obscurity has no doubt been their salvation. Other larger bodies who had secured a measure of official recognition, permission to hold meetings etc., have suffered severely. Meetings have been closed, some have suffered exile, some imprisonment and even death (mostly members of the larger organized bodies). The brethren have not been disturbed since the case in 1925 in Leningrad. Their small numbers, and probably the informality of their gatherings, has been used of the Lord, one feels, to preserve them. They are unable to sing hymns, these are read by a brother, and all that is said is spoken in low voices. But subject to these limitations they are able to break bread, read and pray together much as would be done by brethren elsewhere. No public preaching of the gospel is, of course, permitted.

In Leningrad the pressure is felt still more, owing to the interference with the meeting in 1925. They feel that four or five together is as much as is safe. Our brother Daniel Otsing and our brother P.P. are able to support the saints and to minister to them. Except for one young man from the north east, and visitors from Moscow etc., there are no other brothers. They usually break bread in a couple of gatherings on the Lord's Day. They break bread in the morning, I was told, as most of them are free from work. There are about nine sisters apart from the brothers mentioned. Most of them are elderly. The need of material help is greater here than in Moscow, and most of what is received from abroad is utilized in Leningrad. The Moscow brethren are able to assist too. There is a complete absence of complaint among the brethren, although it might be natural enough in such circumstances. Sending money to them is difficult, but safer if sent to the old ones in Leningrad than in Moscow.

Our brother Daniel Otsing is extremely bright. He is in touch with a number of Christians in Russia who are not with us and must be a light to many in these dark times. He referred to Hosea 2:14-end as indicating the wilderness place, without outward or natural means of sustenance, as indicating the place of isolation where the Lord can sustain His people even in Russia today. The Russians are, of course, naturally fond of organized religion, large companies, ceremonial, hymn singing and so forth. Our brother Daniel Otsing feels that many may be led at this time, when these outward props are taken away, to turn to the Lord in secret. He also referred to Ezekiel 24:15-end, as suggesting the discipline through which the Lord might have to lead His people to bring them to hear the prophetic word.

V.O., the son of our brother D.O., who formerly was with us, is still out of fellowship. It was difficult to ascertain what the difficulty was. He still comes to the meetings at times.

I heard only a little about those breaking bread with us in the north east of Russia and Siberia. They were visited last summer by our brother V. of Moscow. I understand that there are three or four families in Western Siberia, and rather more in the Wjatka district. Our brother F. and his wife are alone in P. in Western Russia. They can only break bread when a visitor comes.

The brethren in Moscow and Leningrad sent their warmest greetings and expressions of love to their brethren in the British Isles and elsewhere, and express their gratitude for the prayers on their behalf.

[Unsigned]

The Letters

1934 to 1958

INTRODUCTION TO A SERIES OF LETTERS CIRCULATED IN 1934

Since our last letters were sent out, authentic details have come to us regarding the deporting of our brethren from Moscow. It appears that a professing Christian had somehow come into contact with our brethren in Leningrad, and for a good while attended the meetings and appeared much interested. From former letters to us, it was a great joy to the few gathered to the Lord there. He was eventually received into fellowship. He afterwards established contact with the saints in Moscow, but he has turned out to be a traitor, probably an agent of the secret police, and has betrayed the brethren. As the saints in Leningrad were mostly aged people, they were perhaps of little service to them, but our two dear brothers in Moscow who are young and fit for work were, after serving a term of imprisonment, sent to labor camps in the far north. Our dear young brother W. almost lost his reason while in prison, but the Lord spared him. His young wife and child, after having sold up their home, have joined him in a room where he is. *(A letter this morning tells us that our sister is back in Moscow again. Why, we do not know – JHL).* The brothers are sent far away from each other, so there is little hope of their meeting each other. How much they both need our prayers. This leaves but one brother in Moscow, who lost a leg in the war. He has a large family to support, and is very poor. He needs our sympathy and prayers. I may also add that our brethren from America who have been there for a long period, returned to this country in time for the conference, and gave us many details of their time with the dear brethren, confirming the news already detailed.

PS While penning this, a line has come to me from our crippled brother in Moscow.

PPS Brethren will remember that in our last notes, we mentioned that sufficient funds were in hand for this year. Our brethren from America who have returned from Russia used something like £50 for the purchase of necessities for the saints during their stay. This we have had to refund them, which has greatly reduced the money in hand. This may appear a large sum, but when we remember that more than two fifths is lost through exchange, it does not leave so much to be divided among the aged and needy. The deportation of our two brothers has also made fresh demands upon the fund. There follow translations of several letters from brethren in Russia.

J.H.Lewis

TRANSLATION OF A LETTER TO MR H D'A CHAMPNEY

Leningrad, 14 March 1934

NOTE: Letter from our aged sister Mrs M., who with her late husband were the first in St. Petersburg to decide to walk with us on my first visit to that city about 25 years ago (c. 1909). She was some years later sentenced to imprisonment for having a few sisters together for a Bible reading, and had to be examined, alone, before the judge, for two hours. The dear brethren gathered all they had together, and just managed to pay the heavy fine in lieu of several months' imprisonment. Next day a letter from England arrived with exactly the same sum of money, sent by the saints for those poor brethren.

H.d'A Champney

My dear brother Champney,

Your dear letter of 4 March I have received. I rejoice that you always remember me with love, as also my dear husband, who has gone home. My husband and I have also often with much love mentioned you. You helped us much to stand in the truth. Your visit was to us a great blessing. In the glory, all will be manifested. We shall see the face of the Lord, and the glory which the Father has prepared for those who have received His Son. I hope and believe that we shall soon see one another in the glory. The days fly like a weaver's shuttle. Also, the years of our life are far advanced. It rejoices me very much that the Lord still gives you strength to serve Him in His vineyard, where there is much work to do. This latter I experienced when in the Autumn I was with my niece in the Caucasus. I had often to think of John 15. The Lord made use of nature as a parable. Now I will close my letter. It will rejoice me from the Lord to receive another letter from you. The brethren send you, and the saints with you, their heartfelt greetings.

Your sister in the Lord

M. M.

A TRANSLATION

My dear S.,   18 March 1934

Today I received your kind letter, full of sympathy. Oh, how loving you are, my dear S. How I should have loved today to have kissed you, and wept upon your breast. You ask whether you could send M. a picture book. No, please don't do this. Also, it is better not to put in any blank sheets of paper in the letter, as it could be misunderstood.

My husband and also J.E. are free there. They had to look for work for themselves. If my husband finds a little room there, I shall no doubt go to him for the summer months, for my husband says it is good in the summer there. A wolf in sheep's clothing came into our flock, and that is why our brothers are over there. They are suffering on account of the Word. My husband wrote to me that, thanks be to the Lord, he is well, only he regrets that they could not find work in the same place, so he has to be quite alone. I do not know how much salary he will receive. He has not been paid up to the present. He could live quite well on the produce, and he has to pay his "ekke" out of this. I have sent him something, then he can buy himself some goods for this. Then he says also that in the eating houses, there is good food obtainable. He even says that if we come, we shall also receive produce and permission to eat in the eating house. F. is of the opinion that this will be sufficient for us. This time, S, I wanted to keep a little more of the brethren's money for ourselves if I get it out here, because it has been sent to me in my name. On the previous occasion we only took a very small part for ourselves. We do not want to take anything at all, but our brothers have ordered this. Otherwise, the one who is really in need is the shoemaker with his large family. He has only one leg, and on this account, he is not able to earn as much as other people. He has 4 children. What he received last time was a great help to him, and he was very thankful to the Lord. There is only this one thing, that he is a weak brother in spirit, and therefore we greatly miss our loved ones. With him it is not possible to speak about everything, as with any other brother.

Greet E., P., and the children very heartily for us. My husband wrote that I was to wait a little longer until a room can be found and then I am to go to him there for the summer. Of course, I should like to take some work into the house, then I need not take M. anywhere. Otherwise there are kindergarten for workmen's children, where the children can stay during the working period, and there also they are fed. Now M. is not accustomed to anything of this kind, to be separated from her mother. Therefore, it is also very hard for me to accept service.

Now with hearty greetings and kisses from M. and myself,
Yours,
L.

PS – I wrote you on the 18th, but I only expect to get to the post tomorrow. M. has a cold, and therefore I cannot get away. I go for bread when she is asleep, and the post is open later, so that it is already too late. Today I received a letter from my husband. He thinks that a room will soon turn up, only it is very expensive there so that he says that we shall not be able to make ends meet with his wages. Well, I have already turned some of my things into money. It will not be enough for the journey, so I must sell some more things, and then all will be well. Do you know, S, what that word is: "Do not be anxious about tomorrow, for tomorrow will care for itself"? Then it is easier for me to look at everything. Do you know, S., it is a reality; I do not know why, but everything seems to me like a dream. Sometimes it seems to me so strange that I have to go so far away and leave the accustomed little nook. It is as though all were going round in my head. I do not know what I had best take with me and what is the best way for me to arrange things. Therefore, it is best for me not to think of anything. Formerly my husband would have looked after all of this. He understands it so well. When we came here at that time after the wedding, it was not at all difficult for us with the removal and the many things. Even at that time it was not easy, but we did it together and in warm love. From the lovely time of youth, there is now only a dream left.

Receive heart greetings from your

L.

TRANSLATION OF A LETTER TO J H LEWIS

My beloved brother in the Lord,   Leningrad, 23 March 1934

It is already known to you that it has pleased the Lord to allow our two dear brothers W. and K, at Moscow, to be banished from their homes, so that only one brother and a few sisters are left there. This brother wrote to me about his present distressing position, saying that he is sick and cannot work as previously. He is very thankful for the gift of love which came to him from you a few months ago through our brother K. He says: "It is hard to say what would happen to him and his family in these distressing times, if it were not for the help of the Lord." He asks us to pray for him, because he is alone without other brothers there. He is a true young brother. He has only one leg, the other he lost in the war, and goes on a crutch. He has a wife and some little children.

We have from our Father now another discipline of His love, which stands in connection with the above. When we received into fellowship here recently another brother, we were convinced that the Lord had sent him to us, and we gave thanks to Him, and hoped that he would be to us even such as Apollos was to the brethren at Ephesus. As they trusted the brother Apollos, so have we here also treated this brother with all love: Acts 18:24-27. The result proved there to be a blessing, but here with us a sorrow — like the act of a traitor. We are in deep humility before the Lord, and accept it, as the other discipline, so also this one as of the Father's 'love and from His hand. We give thanks to Him if He thus forms our spirits, according to the Spirit of Jesus.

Pray for us, dear brother. With hearty greetings from all our dear brethren to the saints who are with you.

Your aged brother in Christ,
Daniel Otsing.

TRANSLATION OF A LETTER TO J H LEWIS.

Beloved Brother in Christ,   Moscow, 6 April 1934

We received your kind letter with thanks. Unfortunately, my husband did not receive the letter himself personally, because he has not been at home since 10 December [*doubtless the time he was in prison — JHL*] but was here for a couple of days, and now he has gone away for a long period. I hope you have already learned some details from my sister. I received your kind letter already long ago, but I only waited to reply as soon as I had received everything because it was in my husband's name and therefore, I could not get it so quickly. He had first of all to send me confirmation. All the brethren thank you and the givers very heartily, for the great love which you are showing to us. We also feel very much that the prayers of the saints, comfort and strengthen us. We are also thinking of all in prayer. That love gift was also received by the brother at the time, only he did not manage to get to reply because he had to go away very soon. Brother K sends his very special thanks. For him it was a very great help. He earns very little with his cobbling and has 4 children. As soon as the Lord gives me the opportunity of visiting my husband, I will also take your letter with me for him. Oh, how lovely it was that summer, when we first became acquainted with one another. The box still stands on the dressing table which you gave me at that time, as a child. How glad I should be to see you again, but that is no doubt quite impossible now. It can only be above, with the Lord.

Yesterday I received a letter from my husband; he has found a room for himself, so that he is already expecting me in April.

Now I am closing with greetings and thanks to all, from us here.

Your sister in the Lord,
H.

TRANSLATION OF A LETTER TO MRS. PAUL COOPER

April 6, 1934

Jesus said, rejoice that your names are written in heaven (Luke 10:10).

My dear sister in the Lord,

I thank you from the bottom of my heart for the nice letter which I received from you some time ago, and also for the comforting thoughts which were in the letter. I wanted to reply very soon, but did not succeed in doing so. In the factory where I work, there is a great deal of work and I must take a big lot home, and then I work through the whole night and in the morning, I must get back to work again. It is true that I need not exert myself so much, but I like to do everything well and in proper time. They do not give me any help, and if I want everything to be in nice order, then I have to work in the evening and many times also in the night — the latter frequently. But I always have to think of the beautiful word in Col 3:23: "Whatsoever ye do, labor at it heartily, as doing it to the Lord and not to men." This word, my dear E.G., is my staff in my service. On this staff I always support myself, though many times tears come into my eyes through weariness.

Although I have not answered you, dear E.G., for such a long time, I was very often with you in spirit. Mother and I think with much warm love of you and your family. How is it with you all? S. has not written to me for a very long time. Perhaps you will be so kind as to send the short letter to S. which I am enclosing.

You would like to know how all the brethren here are getting on. My dear E.G., the two dear brethren who are staying with us here from your side will be able to report to you better. We love this brother and his wife very much. They are very kind. Auntie M. sees them frequently; we however more rarely. But in spirit we are intimately joined with them and pray for them. Auntie M. is at present in good health and sends her hearty greetings. With us, things are as they were of old. Mother looks after the home, and I work. Praise and thanks be to the Lord that He always gives me strength and fresh encouragement. Still quiet and peaceful it is with us here, and every day when I come home from the factory, I find peace and quietness and am received by Mother with love and care, so that I must again and again thank our beloved Lord for His love and goodness.

Dear E.G., I have a great request to put to you. If you should see brother L, or write to him, please give him hearty greetings from Mother and me. He has sent us a parcel — material for a coat — everything that the Lord laid upon his heart was put in with love, and I received a very nice letter from him. I have answered and thank him from the bottom of my heart. Mother and I would greatly rejoice to receive another letter from this brother, because it is so very encouraging. Although I asked brother L. to write again, I did not receive any answer, and do not know whether the letter has reached him.

Dear E.G., I should like to write down one further brief thought which I read today: "But we all, looking on the glory of the Lord with unveiled face, are transformed according to the same image from glory to glory even as by the Lord the Spirit" (2 Cor 3:8). We human beings bear in ourselves unconscious traces of what we are. Those who come from the anvil, the mortar and lime, from the stable and the bam, from the plough and the field, carry the traces of their work with them. If anyone comes home with a basketful of fruit, we observe that he comes from a farm, and if his hands are full of wild plums, we say: "You have been in the fields". How much more shall one who walks with God in heaven through prayer, faith, love and hope, carry in his eyes, in his heart and ways, the holy traces of such a holy intercourse. So just as little as it could remain hidden from the people that Moses had looked upon the face of God for 40 days and 40 nights, just so little can our intercourse with God and our communion with Christ remain hidden. (Exodus 24:18; Exodus 34:35). Anyone who lives in the heavenly atmosphere will carry the odor of this into his surroundings and for the blessing of those around him. These thoughts give me much joy. I am always asking the Lord in quietness to use me more and more in blessing in a quiet way, as also God said to Abraham "and thou shalt be a blessing" (Genesis 12:2).

Now I will close my letter, and will pray to the Lord that He will allow it to get into your hands. Please write to me again very soon. Give my hearty greetings to your family. Mother and I send hearty greetings.

With love, your sister in the Lord,

M.M.

TRANSLATION OF EXTRACT FROM A LETTER TO J H LEWIS.

Dear Brother in the Lord, Leningrad, 12 May 1934

I write to let you know that I have received that which you sent me from the saints on 8 May. Hearty thanks for the same. I received 88 rubles. In May my niece H. came to me. She travelled with her dear little girl to her deported husband, and stayed here a day or two on the way. While with me I had our photographs taken, and send you one as I thought you would like to see them. I am now 61 years old but sustained of the Lord. I will write more next time. 2 Cor. 1:3-4.

My much love and hearty greetings in the Lord, and our heartiest thinks to all, M.M.

TRANSLATION OF A LETTER TO JH LEWIS

Dear Brother Lewis, Leningrad, 20 May 1934

My mother and I thank you very heartily for the letter in which you recorded such beautiful encouraging thoughts. We thank you heartily for this.

We have also received the remittance today, and thank you, dear brother, from our hearts for this gift. We thank the Lord for caring in such a wonderful way in His love for His own, and for the faithful way in which He stands by their side. I have myself translated this last letter, with the Lord's help. It is true it gave me a good deal of trouble, but your letter became still more precious to me on this account, and the thoughts have penetrated still more deeply into my heart.

You speak in your letter, dear brother, of Genesis 15:1 "Fear not, Abram, I am thy shield and thy exceeding great reward".

This verse in the Bible is one of my special favorites — it is so comforting, so encouraging. Often when my heart is heavy, I repeat this verse to myself, but instead of Abram I put my own name. Thus, I feel still more that God addresses this word to me and this always greatly strengthens me. I often think over it when I am alone with the Lord, that as Abram's spiritual condition was good, God was able to speak so much to him and communicate His thoughts to him. Also, our precious Lord Jesus says so beautifully in John 15 v14: "Ye are my friends if ye do whatsoever I command you." God desires that our spiritual condition should become better and better, that we shall become more and more like the Lord Jesus, and this is my earnest, constant prayer to God, that He would in secret make me entirely like His own Son.

Dear brother, if it is possible for you, please write to me very soon again. Mother sends you hearty greetings. We were deeply grieved to have to say goodbye to the brethren S. Now they have no doubt already arrived [in England]. When we bade farewell to each other for the last time, the thought was long in my mind: On earth we shall never see each other again, but perhaps very soon in heaven with the Lord. Please greet the brethren S. and also brother C. from us.

Once more, hearty thanks for your love.

Your sister in Christ,
L.M.

TRANSLATION OF A LETTER TO JH LEWIS

My Beloved Brother,　　　　　　　　Leningrad, July 1934

First of all, I pray your indulgence for keeping you waiting so long for my letter. I had lost my notebook in which I had made some detailed notes owing to my bad memory. Then I have to attend to my daily domestic duties and my old age and infirmities hindered me. I have to limit myself now to what is most essential. The Lord has so willed it.

Your letter 10 July 1934 I received with joy and thanksgiving to God with the enclosed gift of love from the saints of £25, in rubles 145. Praise and thanksgiving be unto the God and Father of our Lord Jesus Christ who has clothed His saints with loving kindness and mercy, having poured His love into their hearts through the Holy Spirit. We send the happy givers our love and thanks, owning our indebtedness and bless you all before God our Father who has so served us in our oppression through the love of Jesus Christ.

Very special thanks to you, my beloved brother, for your letter. Your letters are a great comfort and help to me in my old age in the many tribulation of the last days. The above-mentioned gift of love I have handed to our caretaking brother for distribution. I received as from the Lord through their hands 56 rubles and the balance of 96 rubles has been distributed among the other brethren. We, the receivers of the grace of God, are very happy and thank God for His wonderful care and love. Especially "the brother" thanks the Lord that He has given us to value the thought of care and oversight in the assembly of God. We are still very young in these things and pray our faithful Lord for increased spiritual understanding. We desire first of all to seek the Kingdom of God and His righteousness so that we might know better how to receive and how to give "the added things" and surprises of the Lord as we have even now — Matthew 7 v33; John 6 v27. I continually pray that the Lord may cause all done amongst us to be conducive to the spiritual state of the saints and work out for the glory of God.

Concerning our circumstances, you will have heard by word of mouth from our brethren at S. They have given gifts of love to all the brethren here. We always remember their love and only regret that their visit was so short. Our faithful Lord comforts and refreshes us in our oppression. He has given back to us — "to their own company" and to the fellowship — two of our Wjatka brothers after their many years of trials. They are strengthened in faith and have grown in the knowledge of God and the grace of our Savior Jesus Christ. They sing psalms to their Savior God and we in spirit with them.

The Lord has also added to us here a brother who has grown very slowly. He has been many years with us at the feet of Jesus, a son of consolation. You can only be taught here in this way. We pray continually that God may add to the heavenly host here, many sons of consolation. We Wait for the grace of God which He gave to Paul in his last days — Acts 28:30-31; Rom. 14:17-18 and that we may lead a quiet and peaceable life in all godliness and piety (1 Tim. 2:2; Luke 19:9-10; Rev 22:17; and Psalm 118:15).

Now beloved brother I close with affectionate greetings and God's blessing and love from my sick wife and self to you and your dear wife. Affectionate greetings from all the saints here and much love to all the saints with you.

Yours united in Christ,
Daniel Otsing.

TRANSLATION OF A LATTER TO J.H.LEWIS

My dear brother,   Moscow, 4 September 1934

Heartiest thanks for your kind consideration of me, and for ministering twice for our needs. I have also received your postcard, which I intended answering. The kind gift of the saints, I received from the Lord's hand with joy. Philippians 4:11-13, 18-23. I am enclosing a little photo of my wife, self and our four children. I now close with much love, dear brother, to yourself and your wife, and all the saints from myself and my household.

Your affectionate brother in the Lord,
S. K-h.

The Beautiful Hymn
Written by
Daniel Otsing in 1917

Here is the hymn, as translated.

O Come! Thou, Lord Jesus, we're watching;
And take now Thy spouse home to Thee.
Thine absence awakens deep yearning,
The bride her loved Bridegroom to see.
 Thy heart, O Lord Jesus, is throbbing
With love deep, eternal, we know;
Our hearts in response with love's burning
Await Thee with lamps all aglow.

The Spirit and bride are united
In saying "Come Lord", yea come soon.
Throughout the long night she has waited
To see Thee, her faithful Bridegroom.
Gross darkness the earth doth now cover
And night like a pall shrouds the land.
Thy flock is still here, Shepherd Lover,
The sheep Thou hast kept by Thy hand.

Midst darkness faith clearly sees beaming
The light of Thy coming afar.
We watch for the dawn of the morning,
Blest herald : "The bright morning star".
The word of Thy patience we're keeping;
Its radiancy beams on our path:
Like a beacon us heavenward attracting
To meet Thee: the Hope of our heart.

(more > >)

Oh Lord, with our ears and hearts open
To the sound of Thy trump would we be
The summons that calls us to heaven
For ever to be, Lord, with Thee.
Thy word and The Spirit blest Lover,
As earnest is given to Thy bride,
Thou art near to faith's vision O Saviour
But soon she will be at Thy side.

How sweet is The word "I come quickly".
"Amen!" answer Spirit and bride;
Responsive to love, faithful, holy,
That never has once tumed aside.
Thy promise is sure, blest Protector,
"Not one shall be lost" is Thy word;
Of the men given Thee by Thy Father.
We praise Thee, we bless Thee, O Lord.

Petrograd, 1917 Daniel Otsing

This is the original translation from the German by J.H.Lewis. The wording has been altered for the "Little Flock Hymn Book" and one verse left out.

THE LAST CONTACT WITH DANIEL OTSING

A postcard has reached me from our dear brother

From: Alma Ata, Kazakhstan   3 November 1935

'Dear brother, Through God's grace and love, a new dwelling place has been found for me. We are in good health. Read 1 Peter 1:1-9; Acts 27:1-3; Revelation 1:9; Revelation 22:20-21. My new address is... Write please in German, for I have no translator. Sister... will be returning from me.

Hearty greetings to the brethren.

Your aged brother, D.O.

* * * * *

A further postcard, via Sweden

From: Alma Ata, Kazakhstan   18 November 1935

After my long silence I am writing to you for the second time from my new abode, but receive no answer. I am well and happy, and reading alone in my room the word of God, and pray to God for all men. Philippians 2:20:21; Daniel 9:17-19; 2 Corinthians 7:1; Thessalonians 5:25-26. With hearty greetings to all the saints,

Your loving brother, D.O.

* * * * *

A further postcard -- the last one we know exists.

From: Alma Ata, Kazakhstan   25 November 1935

I am writing to you the third time, and up to the present date have had no answer. You may well think I am not alive, but I am, and in good health, thanks be to God. Read Philippians 1:21; 2 Corinthians 1:8-9. Hearty greetings from me to all the saints,

Your loving brother, D.O.

TRANSLATION OF EXTRACT FROM A LETTER TO J.H.LEWIS FROM ERNA COOPER

Dear Mr Lewis,   Helsingborg, Sweden 2 February 1945

You will be interested to hear that we have had news from Russia. Jenny writes: "I and my daughters are sending our warmest greetings. My son Rudolph is at the front. I am still working as a hospital nurse. We left Leningrad at the end of 1942. We passed through the most difficult and awful time, but with the help of God we are still alive. All our relatives have died through this dreadful war. We have lost all and have had to start life afresh. We are in great need of shoes, clothing, stockings etc. Is dear mother alive? Warmest love and kisses to you all. Greetings to those who remember me." I wrote to my sister in November, so there is hope of her getting my letter. I am thankful to God, Who has heard our prayers, and spared our dear ones. Paul sends his love to you. He is very pressed at business. He will write to you when he can find time.
Our united Christian love
Erna Cooper

TRANSLATION OF A LETTER
FROM MRS. JENNY OTSING
TO HER SISTER, MRS. PAUL COOPER

Leningrad, Sweden, 22 July 1958

"I can only thank the Lord that my health is as good as it is". [She then refers to some nerve trouble and to slight diabetes which she is treating homeopathically, and continues,] I have recently been to a clinic to have my glasses changed. The doctor told me that I have abnormal focus of the eyes, and this gives me headaches and causes me to be easily tired because of strain on the eyes. This has been a thorn for the flesh for me, like Paul, and like Paul I have often pleaded; but I have had to learn to be content with His grace. His strength has been proved mighty by me.

In the hospital where I had worked they had such confidence in me, and I was chosen if there was some special job to be done. Thus, I managed for 25 years; now I am pensioned and am at home, and can rest a little in the afternoon.

I wonder to this day how merciful and gracious the Lord has been, carrying me to this day. Seven years I worked two shifts for two hospital sisters, and often had night duty. If one of the upper people, such as the directors or professors, was ill, I was chosen. That gave me many enemies, but always the Lord stood by me.

I have passed through much with my children. The war came, and my dear Rudie was called up, and was killed in 1943. He loved to pray, and his last words were "Mother, dear, not one of my hairs falls from my head without the will of God." He was a good child, and it was very hard to lose such a one. Gretel has married and has a son. Her husband is always ailing since the war, and works very little. Also, the son is very ill, and cannot stand this damp climate, so she has often to nurse first one and then the other. Lillchen lives with me. God has given me good children but alas, they have forgotten the Lord.

Now I have told you a little about my life. Pray for us; we need your prayers. If you can, would you send me a German Bible in large print. And may the God of peace which passes all understanding keep our hearts and minds in Christ Jesus to life everlasting. I kiss you heartily.

Jenny and Children

COMMENTARIES by Visitors

IMPRESSIONS FROM VISIT TO RUSSIA
Bernt Lindberg, Sweden, following a visit in 1959)

During my stay in Leningrad, I had the opportunity to visit Mrs. Jenny Otsing (a daughter in law of the late Mr. Daniel Otsing). I visited her two Lord's Days and one Monday.

Mrs. O lives in a flat with three rooms, each occupied by different people and they share the kitchen. Her own room is 9 square meters and she shares it with her youngest daughter. There is only place for one bed. I was very heartily received and she was very glad to see a brother. The first thing I did was to assure myself that she did not think it dangerous to receive a visit or to speak freely. She knows German and Swedish besides Russian. She was of good courage and said that I came with the Lord Jesus and then there could be no danger. She also said that if she should get into difficulties, the Lord has a thousand ways to deliver her.

At first I asked a little about her condition and got to know that she had been in prison for five months in 1951 and after that deported for 3 years, being falsely accused of being a spy. There is also another sister, M., at Leningrad of those who were in fellowship when the meeting ceased in 1935. She was in prison for 3 years from 1937 and was sentenced to a working camp for seven years and banned from Leningrad for the rest of her life, as was Mrs. Otsing. But the ban was reversed during de-Stalinisation and they both came back. Mrs. Otsing came first and found M. through enquiring of her relatives.

These two sisters meet alternately in each other's quarters every Lord's Day and break bread. M. had heard from a brother during her exile that when conditions are such that there are no brothers left, sisters could break bread by themselves. I was astonished to hear of sisters breaking bread without a brother and said that we should not do it. I also told her about sisters laying the table while waiting for visiting brothers. Mrs. Otsing had bread and wine in order and asked if we could break bread. I could not say no, so we broke bread two Lord's Days, and I did all I could to encourage her. I brought her the new hymn book, one Swedish and one German copy, and a Swedish, German and Russian Bible. I left it to the Lord to give them wisdom in their wish to remember Him. They meet in greatest secrecy as private meetings are illegal. M. did not show herself at Mrs. Otsing's while I was at Leningrad for reasons of safety. Mrs. Otsing said she was of a nervous nature and I did not insist on seeing her.

The meetings in Moscow and Leningrad ceased in 1935 during persecutions in the instigation of which a false brother had a good part. He was a betrayer and traitor and the brethren have suffered much from false accusations. Practically all the brothers were taken away in 1935 to 1937 and sent to different places, the late Mr. Daniel Otsing was taken at the age of 85 and sent alone to Alma Ata, where he died under very miserable circumstances. The husband of Mrs. Otsing was taken in 1937. Most of these brothers seem to have disappeared and never came back again. Also, sisters were taken. Mrs. Otsing was alone in Leningrad till she found M. After the siege of Leningrad by the German armies (900 days) she was evacuated for recuperation with her two daughters. She also had a son, who was a believer, but he succumbed to a wound in the war. The eldest daughter reads the Bible and is *ein wenig glaubig* [a little believing]. The youngest daughter living at home is not a believer but very kind to her mother. Coming back from the evacuation their quarters had been occupied by others who had stolen their property. These people were turned out by the housing authorities and as a retaliation they reported Mrs. Otsing as a spy. All the brethren were falsely accused as spies, as the constitution does not allow any persecution because of religion, and all their contacts between themselves and brethren abroad were known to the secret police.

Mrs. Otsing told me about many marvelous incidents, how she had proved the Lord's help in a most wonderful way, and about encounters with believers during her work as a nurse. She has had a most remarkable and marvelous history. She remembers the old time and a visit she made to Sweden very well, and longs much for meetings. She also told me about the bringing up of the children and about the difficulties at school. She said that the children of a brother Dr P. are living in Leningrad and are believers. They meet in secrecy with other believers for the reading of the scriptures. She does not know if they break bread. To those people she gives ministry she receives. As to others of those who were in fellowship in 1935, the only ones Mrs. Otsing knows of are the following: a sister and her husband at Kierov; two sisters of whom one is an elderly widow at Krasuojarsk in Siberia. She knows these by correspondence, but she does not know whether they break bread nor much about their spiritual welfare, as they dare not write about such things in letters. Those in Kierov are relatives of Mrs. Otsing's and she hopes to visit them if possible, but the difficulty seems to be accommodation. These people very probably have as narrow quarters as all the others because of the housing shortage. That these are the only ones Mrs. Otsing knows of does not necessarily mean that there are no others left of the brethren. Out of a list of about 40 brethren, 8 are known by Mrs. Otsing certainly to be dead, but at least half of the number must be dead because of old age.

As to believers generally, there are all kinds of sects in Russia, and if there is a number of at least 20, they are allowed to form a religious congregation and have the right to a place to meet. This right however seems only to exist on paper. There is only one evangelical church at Leningrad owned by the Baptists, who are about 3000. However, all other evangelical sects go to this church, so it is visited by about 6000. Recently they got permission to build another church, but shortly after that the permission was withdrawn, probably under the pretext of the housing shortage. It is prohibited to give any religious instruction to children below 18 years of age, and they are not allowed to visit churches. It is very difficult to get any reliable apprehension of the position of believers generally in Russia. But I witnessed things which – quite apart from what Mrs. Otsing told me – shows that there are believers in Russia, and that the Spirit is working there. There are knees that have not bowed to Baal and the Lord knows those that are His in that vast country.

Conditions in Russia are such that it is necessary to pray that our sisters might not come into difficulty by this visit.

ACCOUNT OF A VISIT TO LENINGRAD
Arne Lidbeck, Stockholm, Sweden, June 28-29, 1968

The writer had the privilege and joy of visiting our aged sister Mrs. Eugenia (Jenny) Georgevna Otsing (78 years), daughter-in-law of our brother Mr. Daniel Otsing, writer of hymn 131 in our hymn book.

I found her comparatively well physically, but living in circumstances next to privation, and far from what we would call separate or clean surroundings. In order to understand our sister's dwelling conditions one must know something of what she has passed through during the last war and afterwards. After her husband had left her in unfaithfulness and subsequently died, Mrs. Otsing and her two girls lived by themselves and our sister trained herself to become a nurse. This proved a very useful thing when the German armies besieged Leningrad for 100 days and untold sufferings and calamities ensued. When our sister served at a hospital as a nurse it happened that someone stole her rationing cards, which were of absolute necessity for the maintenance of life. Money was worth nothing. Once the little girls told their mother that they were starving from hunger and had prepared themselves to die, when one day a person in the hospital, whom Mrs. Otsing nursed, suddenly died. She had left a piece of bread in her drawer and Mrs. Otsing took it as from the Lord and gave it to her girls. She herself could get her daily ration (which was utterly scarce) at the hospital. No-one could get hold of a person's rationing cards, which were strictly kept by the head nurse of the hospital. It therefore became a matter of life or death if Mrs. Otsing could or could not get the rye bread left by the persons who died in the hospital. This she gave to her two little girls. During the siege of the German army and its bombardment of the city, one third of all the houses in the city were destroyed or burnt down. All the windows were shattered, and at night when it was coldest the temperature in the room occupied would go down to -15 degrees C. It was a question of using anything and everything to keep from freezing. One leg got frozen once and has given much pain ever since. The children were able to attend school in spite of the siege, during which over 1,000,000 citizens were evacuated.

Once our sister spoke to her children in German and her neighbor overheard her, although he did not understand the German language. He reported Mrs. Otsing to the military authorities. Being a very wicked and evil person, he wanted not only her little flat but also her furniture and belongings. Not having a proper Russian name, she was arrested and sent to Siberia to a small village. Here I must emphasize that it was not at all because of her belief or association with us, as has so often been said, and I do not know who has started such tales that she and others were told to leave Leningrad on that account. Mrs. Otsing and her children were sent to Siberia to a small town in a cattle car. It was in the middle of winter and bitterly cold, but through God's mercy she and the children did not succumb. I think she added that the warmth of the body of a cow helped to keep them sufficiently warm so as not to die. In Siberia, our sister was told to work in a hospital because of her training. Although often really ill, she had to put in partial time at the hospital. Her older daughter was permitted to go south in Siberia and study chemical engineering. She did well and took her graduation there. Mrs. Otsing was allowed to visit her and to stay awhile on account of her good work under most difficult circumstances. Finally, the doctor at the hospital helped her to return to Leningrad with her younger daughter. She returned of her own volition to Siberia for a brief visit.

Her apartment in Leningrad is only 8 square meters (6 ft by 16 ft). The room of her daughter is 13 square meters. Between them is a room of 18 square meters which is occupied by an engineer who shares their kitchen, in which they each have a stove and a wash basin. The toilet room is also shared. When I asked her if she could not possibly change her apartment so as to be freed from the intrusion and inconvenience of the engineer, I was told that her apartment is such that nobody wants it, at least as long as the engineer is there. But Mrs. Otsing also said that engineer had got an offer to move to the Caucasus. As soon as he moves, Mrs. Otsing will try to take over his room. I therefore gave her money so that she could do so without difficulty. In order to get a two room and kitchen apartment she will have to exchange her present one. Otherwise only state, city or military personnel can get priority for newly built apartments. It is impossible to understand or really sympathize with our sister without having been in Leningrad. Our sister has been compelled to help others constantly all through her life and as a result she has also received help in her difficulties. I pleaded, however, with our sister to try to do all she could in order to obtain at least an apartment of her own.

I had with me a Darby New Testament, and ministry by J.T., and "Recovery and Maintenance of the Truth" by A.J.G. in Swedish, and a new Bible in German. I was told just before entering Russia that such books were not allowed to be taken in. I therefore put them together with a Swedish newspaper into an open paper carrier bag and was prepared to ask if I could fetch them again on my return. But the customs officer simply looked at the date on the newspaper, and when he saw that it was of a recent date, he put it back into the bag and let me pass. As Mrs. Otsing knows Swedish fairly well, she was very pleased to get the books. She can read both Swedish and English slowly.

When I asked her if she could not come to Sweden if I furnished her with a return ticket, Leningrad-Stockholm, she replied that she had tried three times to do so, but each time a Russian passport has been denied her despite the fact that her brother-in-law, Mr. Paul Cooper, had obtained a Swedish visa for her. When she asked for a reason for the refusal, she could get no reply, but she thinks that on account of her being once sent to Siberia, the Russian authorities will not want her to relate abroad what she has passed through.

Besides Mrs. Otsing there is only a dear sister by name Lydia Muss and an aged brother by name Fischer who are in fellowship with us, but they are not in Leningrad but away south. Mrs. Otsing is in contact with them through correspondence and, whenever possible, she tries to visit them. Small gifts of clothes can be sent to our sister, but no money. Money can only be given by someone who visits Leningrad, and even so at great discretion. Others who are or were in fellowship with us have been lost or absorbed by the body of Christians who are just identified as Baptists by the State.

The address of our sister and her telephone number can be obtained from Mr. Paul Cooper or myself by anyone who contemplates a visit to Leningrad. Also such information as is of practical use when visiting Leningrad. If any brother or sister would like to know more details, I shall try to obtain them if when I visit our sister again. l shall be glad to go over with a brother if a translator is desirable.

Arne Lidbeck
July 1968

BRETHREN IN RUSSIA

Remembered in 1997

In July 1959 I attended a course in the Russian language arranged by the Swedish people's University in co-operation with the University of Leningrad. It took place at the University in Leningrad and lasted for three weeks. My aim was to find out what had happened to the Brethren during and after the Bolshevik revolution. I had the address of a sister in Leningrad, Jenny Otsing, who was a daughter-in-law of brother Daniel Otsing, 1850-1937, who wrote the famous hymn about the Lord's coming again. I had the address from her sister and brother- in-law, who escaped to Sweden with their family during the revolution.

I wrote a short summary in 1959 [See page 56] about what I learnt from Mrs. Jenny Otsing but for safety and security reasons, Mrs. Otsing did not want to me to disclose certain details in writing for circulation. What I wrote in 1959 for circulation among interested brethren is reproduced here as the first part of this paper. Sister Jenny Otsing has been with the Lord now a long time. Now, 38 years later, some details which may be of interest to brethren who love the Lord's appearing and the hymn of brother Otsing about this great subject, can now be disclosed.

Life in the Meeting in Petrograd and assembly discipline

One interesting question is how the Brethren in Russia could manage to uphold Scriptural principles of separation and assembly discipline during the Kerenski and emerging Bolshevik regimes. Membership of trade unions and voting became gradually compulsory (both not acceptable among the brethren).

One brother could avoid the trade union by being a guilder in a bookbinding enterprise. He was the only guilder in that enterprise, so the guilders trade union was represented by nobody else than himself. Nobody asked if he was a member, which he was not.

Another brother was a solicitor and an active member of a co-operative apartment. He managed to become the officer for renting out. In this way he could provide housing for brethren and for other Christians who had become homeless in the persecution. The brother was not excluded for unholy association.

One brother had paid one rouble to the trade union. Next day a trade union officer came to the brother's home, threatening him with a pistol to pay another rouble for the membership card. The brother said: "I don't bow to the Tsar; I don't bow to the pope, if they infringe on my conscience. I do not decide myself, but my Lord does. So, if you wish to shoot, please do!" The man with the pistol turned back and wished that his faith could have been as strong as the faith of this brother. The brother came from a Polish-Jewish family by name Kubler and escaped later with his family to Sweden. As a refugee he adopted the name Cooper (Paul) and was in fellowship in the meeting in Malmo where I was local as a student.

Some avoided the trade union by working at home. One brother tailored new suits from old by turning the cloth. Another one collected old fat and made soap. And another one started working with jewelry. One brother refused to vote. He reasoned: "They cannot put me to death without a trial (whether this was correct can be questioned: people disappeared without trial) and then I shall have an opportunity to witness for the Lord." Nothing happened before he managed to escape. Another brother voted for Jesus. The next day when the result of the election was presented, the newspaper reported that only one person in Petrograd voted for Jesus. The brother did vote, so he had not broken the law.

One brother was excluded because he refused to buy a sewing machine for his wife, although he could afford it. She was sewing by hand at home. When this came to the knowledge of brother Otsing, he decided they could not have fellowship with the idol of avarice. After a year out of fellowship, the offending brother was restored having handed over the bank account to his wife.

Another brother, who was a river barge skipper, was pricked in his conscience in a bible reading. He had once had to order a new anchor for the shipowner; but he had ordered two, one for a boat of his own. He did not tell his boss and the shipowner paid the bill without noticing that the brother had ordered two anchors and the brother did not pay for his anchor. Now the shipowner was dead and the money could not be restored. The brethren advised the brother to set the money aside for the Lord's work, which he did. But soon after this there was a famine and he used the money for himself and was excluded from fellowship. He was again restored and now he wrote to Mr. H. d'A. Champney in England for advice about how to put the matter right. He did not understand the answer in English and went to a teacher in English for a translation. The teacher refused to accept any payment, but the brother did not feel free to owe anything to a lady who was not a sister in the meeting. "But I am a sister" the lady said. "Well, how do you know that your sins are forgiven?" "This I cannot know before I die". "Then you are not a sister, for our sisters know that their sins are forgiven." This brother distributed relief parcels from brethren in England. Finally, the lady agreed to accept a parcel, and the brother got the letter translated. When he brought the parcel, the lady said that she now knew that her sins were forgiven. How has that come about? Have you been to an evangelistic meeting?" "Yes!" "Did the sisters speak there?" "Yes, they did." "Then you are still not a sister, for our sisters don't speak according to the epistle to the Corinthians." The lady got annoyed and she wrote to Mr. Champney herself asking for an explanation what kind of man had written to the Russian brother, who had such claims on her. Mr. Champney answered in such a wise manner that the lady accepted everything he wrote and became a prominent Plymouth Brethren sister. This lady was the famous Tatjana Stenbock, who in the persecution later managed to escape destitute together with her housemaid to Germany.

The Last Letters
1968 - 1975

Translation from the Russian of the last letter received from our brother Mr Fischer, now with the Lord.

He lived at Biysk, in the Altai Mountains, 2,100 miles south-east of Leningrad and only 300 miles from the border between USSR and Mongolia. The letter was written to Mr. Paul Cooper, whom Mr. Fischer had known for many years since they were together in the meeting in Leningrad in the 1920s.

Beloved brother in the Lord,   Biysk, 27 June 1968

Many years have run their course in this life since the day that we were drawn together to the feet of Jesus and built one another up spiritually in the house of God. But it was the Lord's will to separate us and to set us in different places in distant lands, to be a testimony to Jesus Christ to the end of our days, till the Lord comes.

Many of our fellow-pilgrims of my generation are already at home in the Father's house, seeing the beloved, glorified Jesus at the right hand of God the Father, but I still stand as a tree in the wilderness, surrounded by storm and hail and thunder, but rooted in faith in the Son of God, Jesus Christ, my Redeemer, Who has marked me out for God and prepared a place for me in the Father's house. As it says in John 12 v26, "Where I am, there also shall be my servant."

Beloved brother! Many things have changed in the course of time, but who will separate us from the love of God? Tribulation, or distress, or persecution, or famine, or nakedness, danger or sword? (Romans 8 v31-35). "If God be for us, who against us?". "But in that I now live in flesh, I live by faith, the faith of the Son of God, Who loved me and has given Himself for me". (Galatians 2 v20.)

As to what pertains to my daily life, I sum it up in the words of Isaiah 40:29-31, "He giveth power to the faint; and to him that hath no might He increaseth strength. Even the youths shall faint and tire, and the young men shall stumble and fall; but they that wait upon Jehovah shall renew their strength: they shall mount up with wings as eagles; they shall run, and not tire; they shall walk and not faint".

With warm love to you and all the saints

Your affectionate brother, G. Fischer.

Translation from German of a letter to Mrs Alice Mutton

My dear Alice,   Leningrad, October 10, 1975

Thank you very much for your letter. Thank you also for thinking about me, your old Aunt. For we haven't seen each other for about 70 years! You were still a little girl when we parted from your family. I am surprised that you still know the German language so well. I have quite forgotten Swedish, but I can still recite a Swedish verse. When I went to the Swedish school at eight years old, my favorite lady teacher wrote in my album. I haven't forgotten it to this day although I'm just about 86 years old.

Do you want to know how I am getting on? Well, I am getting on well now, although I have gone through much — many difficulties all these years. I have 3 children. My son was killed in the war. My oldest child, Margaret, is already a grandmother, so I am a great grandmother. My youngest, Elsbeth, is unmarried. I live with her, run the little household etc., but everything goes very slowly. My feet are very weak and I forget everything.

Yes, soon we shall all meet with our Lord Jesus, that is our hope in this world.

Now I must close. Greetings to your husband and greetings and kisses to yourself from Aunt Jenny.

Jenny Otsing

(Mrs Jenny Otsing was a sister of Mrs. Paul Cooper, mother of Mrs Alice Mutton.)

* * * * *

Letters from Lydia Muhs to Paul and Sonja Cooper

Lydia lived in Karaganda, some 2,000 miles South East of St Petersburg.

December, 30 1967

I thank you and Paul heartily that you continually think of me before the Lord. Your love for me is most precious to me. Your photo, Sonja, is just above my pillow and I always look into your dear friendly face and to me it is as if I hear your voice saying, "As are thy days, so shall thy strength be." This is like a staff in my weary hand. Do pray for me my dear Sonja. My age rests heavily upon me. Greet Paul heartily from me. I embrace you my very, very dear Sonja,

Lydia.

* * * * *

My dear Sonja,   September 24, 1968

Hearty greetings to you and Paul and thank you for thinking of me. It is very precious to me to think that in far off lands there are dear loving brethren thinking of me and praying for me. My dear Sonja, my moving to another apartment is drawing near, but I will again have other people living there and will not be able to be alone. But this I have already for a long time spoken about to the Lord, that He Himself will choose my neighbors and that He will bless my move out of here after 4 years, and bless my move into another room....Oh how difficult, how difficult and hard is the way that our Blessed

Lord has chosen for me. If you could only for one moment see my neighbors when they are drunk, you would understand everything...

Lydia

* * * * *

Extracts from two letters from Mrs Jenny Otsing to Paul and Sonja Cooper

July 25, 1972
...I was twice evacuated to Siberia. The Lord allowed that evil doers should act, but He protected me and has not given me up and was with me. To him be glory!

...and now I am waiting for the Lord to come and to take me. Be vigilant praying at all times. Soon our Lord shall come to fetch those who wait in prayer to the heavenly supper. Wait, pray, the Lord so commands, soon He comes in glory and takes us where the light is shining...
Jenny Otsing

* * * * *

February 1, 1973
...Churches and meetings do not exist over here, I am entirely alone.

...O my Lord, Thou hast given Thy life for me, how shall I not give my life to Thee...

I must close now with greetings to all in the house, and the peace of God which surpasses every understanding, shall guard your hearts and your thoughts by Christ Jesus for the eternal life.
Jenny Otsing

[Mrs. Jenny Otsing is 82 years old.]

MISS STENBOCK'S CONVERSION
(as related by herself)

<u>Historical note:</u> *Our sister was the daughter of Count Stenbock who was heir to the estates at Kalk, Estonia. From 1940 most of her life was spent in a displaced persons camp in Germany.*

The following account of personal experiences might begin with the explanation that the Russian word for "monk" means "that which is different". Over the whole of my life I could write these words "It all came differently", and I may add that, by Divine mercy, it came far better than could in any way have been expected under the given circumstances as will I hope be seen from the short narrative below. My God had His own thoughts for me, and being indeed the God of circumstances, He overruled everything perfectly, and brought the result which He had willed from the beginning. Born of parents of noble birth, in the lap of luxury.

I was a disappointment to my parents from the very first, for instead of being the expected heir to my father's estates, I was born a girl, and owing to an accident, that even the skillful physician who attended my mother could not prevent, I was lame from birth. However, what seemed to be a misfortune at the time, proved to be a God given safeguard against many dangers I would most probably have incurred in the world. I have learned to be particularly thankful for these limitations. My dear grandmother, who was a sincere and devoted Christian according to her light, as endorsing the doctrine and practice of the Greek Orthodox Church, brought me up under the influence of all that is best in that religion, reading the New Testament, and the lives of the saints to me, taking me to all the churches in St. Petersburg where I lived with her while I attended school, and her fondest wish was, that I should become a nun. My youthful mind was filled with idealism, my heart burned for a life of self-sacrifice and devotion to the poor, and the quiet ecstasy of praying in dimly lit temples, fragrant with incense, and resounding to the strains of the most beautiful singing I had ever heard, satisfying my longing for Worship.

So, I seemed to be on my way to becoming a very genuine nun, "but it all came differently". At about twelve years of age I began to ask questions; I began by asking information from the priest who taught us Catechism at school, but he only wanted us to learn things by heart, and I daresay, I often annoyed and perplexed him with my insistent wish to know, and to understand. I then turned to my grandmother. I wanted to know why our life was so different from the lives of the saints, whom she had taught me to admire and reverence, and why we did not act more on the Lord's words in Matthew 19:21 "If thou wouldest be perfect, go sell what thou hast, and give to the poor, and thou shalt have treasure in heaven, and come follow me". As a matter of fact, I was beginning, not only to be sorry for the poor, and destitute, but to be heartily ashamed of our opulence, and when, after church service was over, I was given a handful of pennies to give the beggars waiting outside the church portals, I could not bring myself to look upon their faces. Once I was severely reprimanded for suddenly kissing a little beggar child, with pathetic eyes, and all trembling with cold, and was well scrubbed in a hot bath afterwards for fear of dirt and germs And yet, had not the deeds of pious men been held up to me as an example, of such, as had not only served lepers, but had kissed their sores.

I was puzzled and disheartened, and gradually lost my childish fervor, not finding anything definite to replace it. I grew up with rather vague aspirations to adhere to the Sermon on the Mount and thought I was a practicing Christian. However, I felt dissatisfied with myself all the time, I did not know I was trying to do a hopeless thing, I was endeavoring to perfect myself, and did not know that I had to be displaced instead, judged to be utterly worthless in the light of the Cross, and buried out of sight in baptism. I had never once heard the glorious Gospel of the new Man where righteousness is accounted ours by faith in His accomplished work. The church I belonged to did not teach that at all, I have only lately come to understand in what a dangerous state I then was, for my "house" having been more or less swept and garnished by a religious upbringing, and being empty of the occupant who alone sanctifies and hallows our inner being, I might have fallen an easy prey to quite another kind of idealism.

A short time after I had left school Lenin arrived in St. Petersburg, setting fire to all the evil lusts of the crowds that assembled to hear him propound his gospel of freedom, which was to be brought about by murder and vengeance. Millions were deceived by the seemingly brilliant Theory of Communism, but for me, by mercy, this too, came quite differently. Before I had time to attend a single political meeting that was then being held at every street corner, I was invited by a friend to go and hear something that was quite new to us at that time; in fact the friend said, she had never heard anything so strange and new before, and wanted me to come and hear it too. It turned out to be a young Christian, who was standing before a very mixed multitude in a big public hall. It was the first Gospel preaching I had ever heard, and I will never forget it. Outside in the street the sound of rushing feet of the clash and clatter of shots and breaking glass, of angry voices and hoarse and piteous cries, "the voice of the people", which as the Russian saying goes is "the voice of God".

Inside the hall a part of the same crowd, listening intently with bated breath, and with a fierce and hungry longing in which lurked a challenge, and a demand to what that unknown quiet eyed young man could have to say at such a momentous crisis. It seemed that if he disappointed or failed them, he would be mercilessly swept away by the surging multitude outside, that was meeting out justice below. He spoke of Lazarus, of death in trespasses and sins, of the process of corruption and degradation of the invisible power of our arch enemy, sin, and its consequential death. His assertation that the earth stank with blood, needed no other substantiation than the sounds that reached us from the street below. The devastating effects of the fury of vengeance of murderous hatred, were all around us, a danger not to be forgotten for a moment. He then put the pertinent question, "Is it too late?" It was indeed a question of life and death, and he put it again and again. Then he proclaimed the glorious gospel of the Son of God, whose quickening voice raises the dead. He, so to speak, put us alongside the Son of God, watching in faith, and the sure hope of seeing the glory of God in resurrection in the swallowing up of death in victory. This word preserved me from politics for the rest of my life, and when years later a prominent Communist tried to persuade me, and flatter me into going with them, I was emboldened to refute his assertion that the practice of Christianity and Communism were almost identical by pointing out that those two doctrines were opposed to each other, for does not the Communist say to every man, "Thou rogue, all that is thine is mine", while the approach of the Christian is, "Brother, all that is mine is thine".

To my sorrow, I was obliged to return to Estonia in 1919. Here I led a happy and busy life, having lost all my earthly possessions, and working hard to maintain myself and some loved ones. I felt the tragedy that was happening in Russia keenly, and wished I knew what to do to stand for truth and righteousness at such a terrible time.

Then it was, I heard my second Gospel preaching. A well-known evangelist, exiled from Russia, came to Estonia. I felt I could trust this man, for he had come from the burning house next door, so to speak. He had acted in faithfulness and love, and he had come to us with an urgent message. This man would be able to tell me what to do, so I went to him with a whole list of questions, hoping to find guidance for a better and more useful life, but it all came out different. When I told this dear man of God what I had come for, he pointed me to John 6:29, "What should we do to work the works of God?" "This is the work of God, that ye believe on Him, whom He has sent". When I said I believed, he asked me whether I believed He was now risen and lived? On hearing that I believed this, he asked me a very simple question, which however, put me in the presence of the One whom I professed to believe, yet did not know: "If you indeed believe Him to be alive, why do you ask me, a mere man, what to do, instead of asking Him?" This was quite unexpected, such a thought had never once occurred to me, and I was overjoyed at such a possibility. After a very earnest talk, we both knelt to pray. My prayer was simple, a mere child might have uttered it, but the result was wonderful. Rising from my knees, I was filled with such unutterable peace, such festive joy, as if I had heard Him whose face I had come to seek, say His solemn and conclusive Amen to my prayer for acceptance.

Next day, I heard the same man preach the gospel from the word, "I am my beloved's and my beloved is mine, He feedeth His flock among the lilies; set me as a seal upon Thy heart as a seal upon Thine arm, for love is strong as death". This word became the keynote of my Christian pathway, when the Lord Himself became my Song of Songs. For about two years after I was in touch with many dear Christians of different denominations, I did not yet enquire into the differences between the various denominations, taking it for granted, that sectarianism was unavoidable on this earth.

When I first heard of separation from evil, I misunderstood its meaning, and thought it might involve separating from and renouncing brethren, true Christians, many of whom had sealed their fate by martyrdom. Then we were visited in Estonia by those who held the truth of the assembly of God. They took great pains with me and never tired of expounding the truth to me in the most enlightening way. But I had got a wrong thought into my head and was on the way to endorsing the foundation on which the Alliance movement, and the Free Christian group stand, but it all came differently. One blessed day, I was arrested by the words, "Tell me, thou whom my soul loveth, where Thou feedest Thy flock, where Thou makest it rest at noon, for why should I be as one veiled beside the flocks of Thy companions". Why indeed I asked myself, as the difference between being with the flock of the Good Shepherd, as over against the flocks of

Thy companions, began to dawn on me at last. Then and there, wholly ignoring all denominational questions, I prayed fervently to the One "Whom my soul loveth" to show me the true way, to show me how to act in the light of the wonderful principle the Spirit intimates, in the above-mentioned words. The answer came in power, and at once all became clear and simple, for I was given to see what I had never seen before, the glory of the bride the Lamb's wife. He who hath the bride is the bridegroom. What a bride it behoved Him to have? I have since been told by one who visited me not long ago that it is as much a gift of sovereign mercy to see the bride as a whole, cherished and undefiled, the one pearl of great price, as is new birth and conversion.

One thing I am certain of, no amount of the most enlightening ministry would have led me right through the maze of confusion, as having understood and judged all the existing errors. It was a direct revelation from Christ, or might I say, rather His confirmation of the ministry presented to me, that brought me right into the light, and clear of sectarian grounds. Oh the difference it made, I was clear of man's organization of ecclesiastical congregations, of all that man has built up, to claim as his religion or as that of his Father's. I had not yet fully realized, that I had come into the realm of Divine operations, but I was already learning to loose the sandals from off my feet (the sandals in which man-made customs and religions find a standing), as it behoves us to do when treading on holy ground. I repeat that I did not learn the truth by comparing and judging of the various denominations, but, "Beholding the Lamb of God", and His absolute right to all those He had bought by His precious blood. They were bought with a price, and were his to do with as He liked. What denomination could stand in the face of the prayers of the One who was going to give His precious life for the flock, as He prayed, "That they may be all one, as Thou Father art in me, and I in Thee that they also may be one in us, that the world may know that Thou hast sent me, and the glory which Thou has given me I have given them, that they may be one". Do you see the glory of that unity?

The glory of it, "I in them, and Thou in me, that they may be perfected into one, and that the world may know that Thou hast sent me, and that Thou hast loved them as Thou hast loved me".

I verily believe that the Devil's masterpiece is the erroneous notion that he has spread among large Christian circles that the unity of the bride is mystical, that it is unseen, and even, that it is not meant to be seen on earth at all. Many true Christians hold this erroneous notion, thus missing the import of the real and living presence of Christ's assembly on earth. If the Lord Himself stipulates that the believing of the world depends on its seeing our unity, how can it be according to His will that the unity of the assembly should not be seen on earth? The Devil keeps suggesting that this way is too narrow for enlightened Christians giving no room for love to expand. But how narrow is it exactly?

It is limited by the death of Christ, solemn consideration, and rightly excludes everything that is extraneous to the body of Christ. Our movements must be in keeping with what is involved in the precious body that was given for us. How are we regarding it? Do we distinguish the body? May we not say that many Christian's bodies have become weak and infirm, and a great many are fallen asleep, because of a disastrous lack of discernment as to the body? May the thought of the crown of thorns worn by the Lord Jesus upon the cross help us to judge all the workings of our natural minds, giving place to the mind of the Spirit. The truth is precious for He himself is the truth, and He is love. The truth is not against any of the members of the body, to whatever denomination they may happen to belong, for He who is the truth died for every single one of them. But the truth is against denominations as such, as dividing the truth of the body. Let us seek the truth on our bended knees. When found, it will neither disappoint or fail us for it is the Lord Himself.

Dear fellow Christians, have you heard the midnight call? The word the Spirit has especially been bringing to our notice for the last 200 years, "Behold the bridegroom". It is not only that the bridegroom is coming, but it is His greatness and glory, that is presented to our enraptured gaze. And, are you aware of the greatest movement that is taking place on earth, right now, and every day? It is the service of the blessed Spirit of God, who is occupied with furthering Christ's greatest interest on earth, the bride. He is wooing her, attracting and leading her, guiding her through the wilderness, speaking comfort to her on the way, teaching her to know and love and reverence her Head, who has been given to her, as head overall. He is teaching her to treasure Him, as a bundle of myrrh between her breasts, during the night of His rejection. He is showing her His cheeks, that were smitten for her, and she sees them as beds of sweet plants. He is unveiling the mysteries of the love of Divine Persons, the Father's joy in His Son – His bride. The Lord's joy in presenting His bride to the Father, and in the face of the transcendent glory of Their mysteries, and in what they involve for her. She is learning to veil herself, to live wholly to Him, a spring shut up, a fountain sealed, and even more wonderful, she is growing aware of being an entity, with a new self-consciousness, for the Spirit tells her that in the eyes of her Beloved she is a narcissus of Sharon, a lily of the valleys. The Spirit enables her to hear the voice of her Beloved, "Arise my love, my fair one and come away. My dove in the clefts of the rock, in the covert of the precipice. Let me see they countenance, let me hear thy voice, for sweet is thy voice and thy countenance is comely." Are you aware of this entity? Do you echo the query, "Who is this, she who cometh up from the wilderness, like pillars of smoke perfumed with myrrh, and frankincense, with all the powders of the merchant?" If so, it is high time to hasten, and loose the sandals from off your feet for you are entering the realm of Divine operations and this is indeed hallowed ground.

Tatjana Stenbock

Letter Concerning Tatjana Stenbock --

Gothenburg, Sweden   August 24, 1989

When she left Estonia she visited our brethren in Stockholm. I believe she might have been allowed to stay, but chose rather to be together with the poor ones and moved to Germany.

The camp was not far from Hamburg, and on our way home from England 1955 we decided to visit her as we were to spend a week end in Hamburg. A brother in England who knew her well sent a gift with us to her when he heard about our desire to see her. We drove to the place, it looked so dreadful and poor. She had a small room together with a believer who had followed her the whole way from Reval (Tallin. Estonia). She was grateful to be in the place available for the Lord, to speak about Him to the poor ones in the camp with whom she shared most of what she got from the brethren. She had no intention to seek a better place. She got ministry from England.

You may wonder how she came in contact with our brethren. [See her autobiography page 71.] I can remember from the twenties that Estonia was visited by our brother Mr. J Lewis from Swindon, later by Mr. Arthur Sheddon from Wallshall, Birmingham together with Paul Cooper. Two brothers from Gothenburg visited them with food during the starvation times after the first world war.

I believe that JT's ministry (about an isolated sister being right in arranging the Lord's supper when she had visiting brethren on the condition that she was able to act in discipline if needed) that he had in mind what happened in Reval, when Miss Stenbock had the sorrow but courage to withdraw from the only local brother.

This is how it happened. On her way to the supper one Lord's Day she met this brother and she happened to quote Psalm 25:3 "Who shall ascend into the mount of Jehovah? and who shall stand in his holy place? He that has blameless hands and a pure heart." The brother was struck in his conscience and confessed he was in sin and unable to break bread, and she had to withdraw from that only brother in the meeting.

As to my personal contact with her I only saw her once, and that was in that camp near Hamburg. It did not seem that the local brethren there cared much for her. The great impression I had was, how content she could be under those poor circumstances. Her satisfaction was in spreading the gospel and sharing her supplies with the poor. I close with love in our Lord Jesus in which my wife joins.

Yours affectionately in Him, Kjell Lidbeck

Notes of Readings in St. Petersburg

---oooOOOooo---

THE GENERATION OF FAITH

26th April – 2nd May 1911 (Old Style, Julian calendar)
6th – 15th May 1911 (New Style, Gregorian calendar)

on the occasion of the visit of
P.R. Morford and P. Jensen
from London

THE GENERATION OF FAITH
The faith once delivered to the saints
Jude 1-4; Luke 18:1-8

In Luke 18:8 we read the Lord's solemn and exceedingly important question: "But when the Son of man comes, shall he indeed find faith on the earth?" *The* faith (German translation). We desire to learn today how we can be preserved in the faith. It is an important fact that we are *preserved in Jesus Christ* (Jude 1) and not in ourselves. We are the called ones, who are preserved in Jesus Christ. We are saved by Him and preserved in Him. It is furthermore remarkable that it says: We are preserved "in Jesus Christ" and not in "Christ Jesus" – because we are preserved in His Person – in Him, the Man, who walked here before God day and night in lowliness and dependence. (See Psalm 16:1, "Preserve me, O God: for I trust in thee.") The Lord's life was a continuous prayer, and therefore our lives should also be like a prayer, our whole conduct should be dependent on the Lord. It is only in this Man – in Jesus Christ alone – that we can stand before God. The Man Jesus Christ is so exalted, that all other men have been done away with through His cross; only He alone can stand before God. – The "called ones beloved in God the Father and preserved in Jesus Christ" (Jude v.1) are those that are a new creation. That Man was out of heaven, not out of the earth. He was the Son of God, who came down to the earth as Man in a bondman's form. He was on earth as a Man of a totally different order, the second Man out of heaven, not out of the earth, He was spotless, pure and holy. Everything for us is founded on the basis of His death, we have no part with Him otherwise. There is a difference between being "preserved" and being "kept" (Jude v.1 and v.6). Being kept stands here in contrast to being preserved. Both are in the hand of God. Verse 6 deals with sin, as does 2 Peter 2:4. We have apostasy here. Believers are preserved in Jesus Christ, the apostate are kept to the judgment. There is only *one* Man in the whole universe who could leave His place without becoming apostate. Apostasy was impossible for Him. "Their sorrows shall be multiplied that hasten after another: [...] I will not take up their names into my lips" (Psalm 16:4). He never took up the name of another god into His lips. The saints must never give room to the god of this world in any way. ... The Lord has a goodly heritage (v. 6). His own, the saints, are His inheritance. ... "Mercy to you, and peace, and love be multiplied" (Jude 2). There is growth in the saints – ever "more and more." *We are responsible to preserve* **the** *faith* – the faith once delivered to the saints – so that, when the Son of man comes, He finds *this* faith (Luke 18:8). Where shall He find it? Each one of us is to answer this question, as each one of us is responsible for it. The enemy – Satan – hates the Christian faith and seeks to "tear it to pieces," as one "tears apart" (breaks) the links of a chain, so that they cannot be chained together anymore. Not only does he seek to *destroy* the faith, but to *tear it to pieces*, so that the chain of faith cannot be joined or "chained together" anymore. The chain of faith is linked to a Person – indeed the whole of Christianity *is a Person*, i.e. "the Man Jesus Christ"; it is not a "religion", that is what Christendom has made this Person.

1 John 2:28: "And now, children, abide in him, that if he be manifested we may have boldness, and not be put to shame from before him at his coming." "See to yourselves, that we may not lose what we have wrought, but may receive full wages" (2 John v. 8). "*We*" in this passage refers to the apostles, but the saints are "built upon the foundation of the apostles and prophets, Jesus Christ himself being the corner-stone" (Eph. 2:20). How can we contend earnestly for the faith once delivered to the saints? – We find the answer in Jude 20 and 21: "But *ye*, beloved, building yourselves up on your most holy faith, *praying in the Holy Spirit*, keep yourselves in the love of God, awaiting the mercy of our Lord Jesus Christ unto eternal life." Our panoply is described in Ephesians 6; for if we want to combat, we need to be armed. The Christian panoply has been given to the company, but each one of us must possess it for ourselves. The panoply consists not only of a sword, but *the complete armour belongs to it*. The most important thing is prayer and supplication

in the Spirit. – In Ephesians 6:18 we see once again the dependence of the Lord Jesus Christ, like in Psalm 16, which is to be found here in the saints, too. There is no armour for the back; therefore, believers should not be cowards, but stand up against the enemy courageously, for if you turn your back on the enemy, you are exposed to the darts of the wicked one. We should always move forward. "The panoply of God" (Eph. 6:11, 13) is designated by the Greek word "panoplia"; this word includes the whole armour. Therefore put on, "take to you" the panoply of God. ... Some only fight with the sword, and that is why they are defeated. In Acts 19 we see those who meet the enemy only with the sword, but they are not recognized by the enemy. He says: "Jesus I know [...]; but *ye*, who are ye?" The consequence of that was that they were overcome and defeated, so that they fled naked and wounded; they had taken on just a part of the panoply of God. In contrast to the panoply of God for the believers in Ephesians 6, we find in Job 41 a remarkable description of the armour of Satan. No one but God can vanquish the foe – Satan. Once we have acknowledged the importance of having taken on the whole panoply of God in order to contend earnestly for the faith once delivered to the saints (Jude 3), it will become indispensable for us. The panoply serves two purposes: to protect and to attack. Only the sword is meant for attacking, the rest of the panoply is for protection. Prayer (Eph. 6:18, 19) is the most important part of the panoply. Prayer implies complete confidence in God. Just like a soldier has to confide completely in his superior, his appointed leader, so we, too, must surrender wholly to the Lord. We can be certain that the longer we are on earth, the stronger and fiercer the enemy's attacks will be. He will always leave a lukewarm Christendom alone. He does not need to destroy anything there; it does not hinder him. But we have to contend, because we meet the enemy's opposition every moment. As soon as the saints give Satan a little room, they stop combatting; but to be faithful to the faith once delivered to the saints, the combat should not cease. It is surely worthwhile. Christ suffered for us, He gave *His life* for us. If our faith had merely a religion as its object, it would be worthless, but *it has a Person as its object*, who is worth more than anything. The Lord loves us, and we do not want to deny Him. Many are willing to acknowledge Him as Saviour, but not as their "Master" (2 Peter 2:1). He is *our only Master*, our Master and Lord (Jude v. 4). – Jude verse 9 contains important teaching for us. Michael, the archangel, said to the enemy: "*The Lord* rebuke thee," and leaves all to the Lord. He does not want to act by himself. That is a very noteworthy instruction; we often act differently when we see Satan at work. We want to stand up to him *ourselves*. It should not be so; we should leave it to the Lord. "The Lord rebuke thee."

When the Son of man comes, shall He find faith, the Christian faith, that has been delivered to us to be preserved? To whom has this faith been delivered? To the saints. To what end? That the saints might preserve it. Now, am I allowed to abandon this faith? It has been delivered to us, it is our privilege, and we are responsible to contend earnestly for it – for this faith *once* delivered to the saints. What a great and wonderful privilege God has entrusted to men!

Some Thoughts on Baptism

We find baptism – the Lord's baptism, baptism in the family of God – in the Old Testament in many types and presented from various perspectives. In the New Testament we find the *doctrine of baptism*. We learn the principles of baptism by contemplating the lives of the patriarchs, of Noah, Abraham and Moses, and also in the passage of the children of Israel through the Red Sea, and in circumcision. We see furthermore that God considers the believer as one with his house. Of course, *faith* is *closely linked* with baptism, and so it is a means of maintaining the generation of faith. "But when the Son of man comes, shall he indeed find faith on the earth?" (Luke 18:8)

Satan has always attempted to wipe out the generation of faith on earth. Thus, Pharaoh wanted to kill all the Israelites' male children – the generation of faith in the old covenant (Exodus 1 and 2), but the faith of a man from the house of Levi led him to take a daughter of Levi as his wife and to continue the generation of faith (Exodus 2:1). The same faith of the parents also finds means and ways to maintain this generation of faith. But for that, the child had to be put into the water – in one word, "given over into death." Satan had commanded through Pharaoh that every new-born son of the children of Israel had to be thrown into the river. Why every *son*? Satan's attempt, which we can find all throughout Scripture, is *to destroy the "promised Seed" – Christ*, and that is still his aim today.

There could not be a more dangerous place for the little boy. A sure death threatened him here. But it was exactly here that the child had to be brought. We see the same aspiration of Satan when the Child Jesus had been born. He tried to exterminate the generation of faith through Herod's command. But God is greater than the power of the enemy, and faith acts for God – it does not even consider the power of the world, and God gives our children back to us; that is to say, the children that we, in faith in Him, have given over into death; He gives them back so that we might nourish and raise them for Him. In Pharaoh's daughter we get a figure of God's care and His power watching over everything. She calls the child "Moses", i.e. drawn out of the water, and thus puts on him the true name of every Christian. The mother receives the child to nurse it. She feeds it, and thus the generation of faith is preserved.

Just like the children of Israel had been baptised unto their leader Moses (1 Cor. 10:2), thus we are baptised unto our Leader and Lord Christ Jesus (Rom. 6:1-8), "in order that, even as Christ has been raised up from among the dead by the glory of the Father, so *we* also should walk in newness of life." Baptism holds for all that belongs to the Lord, it is a privilege and not a commandment, just like the supper is a privilege and not a commandment. There are only two privileges in Christianity that are expressed by Christian acts: baptism and the supper. And for us, responsibility is closely connected with both privileges – with baptism and the supper. Baptism is done for God and it holds for God.

Baptism is done to me and for me; no one can baptise himself. It is a sign that I have died with Christ and have been put away from this scene. Baptism signifies not only death, but burial. I cannot bury myself either, nor can I baptise myself. A Christian is under the obligation before God to have his whole house baptised. Baptism is done for God. It should not be a public display, but it should certainly be done in Christian fellowship. My children are my own "I", "I myself", and now I present my own to give them over into Christ's death. Baptism means separation – but at the same time it is a figure of salvation through water, the passage from one world into another; for Christianity is not earthly, it is heavenly.

How great is the heart of God! He saves not just individual souls, *He saves the man and his house.* Thus, baptism applies to the whole family, yea, what is more, to the whole household, it applies to all that belongs to the Lord. We see this clearly at the beginning of the assembly in Philippi. People call us "paedobaptists". This designation is not accurate. Scripture says (Acts 16:15, 31) "thou and thy house." Faith wants to preserve its household, the generation of faith. Faith in God is to be preserved with our children, so that later it can become operative in them and, when they themselves start to understand, it will be realised by them.

Eph. 6:1-3. When children are obedient, they have made a good start in the first relationship into which God has brought them, and they will be better qualified to maintain the faith when it is their turn. We see that when the children of Israel left Egypt – Egypt is a figure of this world – they did not leave their children behind. When I myself have been saved from the world, I must not leave my child back in the world. Speaking figuratively, baptism is the greatest lever parents can apply for their children's upbringing. Of course, parents should not for this reason be negligent in raising their children. Baptism does not release them from their responsibility; on the contrary, it increases it, and this responsibility towards God lasts as long as we live. In 1 Cor. 15:29 we even read about baptism for the dead. The generation of faith is like an army in that sense: the first rank falls, the second marches forward in its stead.

It is very solemn to think that the whole nation has been baptised in the Name of the Father, the Son and the Holy Spirit, that it now stands on the ground of responsibility, that it is responsible when it rejects the Word of God. But only faith can realise what baptism means (Rom. 6:17, 1 Peter 3:10-22 and 4:1-6). Christian baptism is performed "in the Name of the Lord Jesus Christ."

Ever since Christ was unjustly convicted, there is no justice in this world any more. The world will be purged through judgment, and the Christian anticipates a new world. But in this time already as Christians we stand under the administration of God and if we walk in the pathway of faith we can live and see good days (1 Peter 3:10).

These good days certainly stand in no relation to this world, but to a world on the other side of death, that has been brought to light by the death of Christ and in which we live by faith already now. That world is future, but *it belongs to faith already now*. If we see this, we shall gain an understanding of how to walk as Christians here, in order to see or have "good days" according to God's estimate. And thus, we see in 1 Peter 3 from verse 10 onwards how the righteous are to conduct themselves. Christ is sanctified in our hearts, recognised as Lord in our hearts, and so we find in a measure in our own hearts the fortress to which we can flee, namely Christ. In John 10 we see Him as the good Shepherd going before His sheep, and how they follow Him and hear His voice. He speaks in such a way that we hear His voice and can distinguish it from all other voices. He speaks to me, to you, to each one of us (see John 10:11, 17, 28, 29, 30).

* * * * *

On Christian Marriage

(1 Corinthians 7)

In this chapter, the apostle distinguishes between two things: those things that the Lord had commanded him and those that he considered right according to his own estimate. He speaks spiritually, but wherever he gives a commandment he says it is a commandment of the Lord. He distinguishes between revelation and inspiration. It was God's will that the apostle should write in this way, so that there is order in all things, and thus we have received knowledge of how to conduct ourselves in marriage and what attitude to take towards it.

Verse 23. We have been "*bought with a price*" out of this world *for God*; man is not for himself and woman is not for herself, but for God; this thought should govern us.

The first relationship God gave to man was marriage; it was given indeed *before sin came into the world*. Before the incoming of sin into the world, there was no other relationship apart from marriage; it is the only figure of Christ's relationship to His bride and stands, therefore, wholly beyond the question of sin.

In the pagan world, the creature is placed over God. All bonds were destroyed and ruined, and this was especially the case in *Corinth*, a licentious city. But the light of Christ exposed everything, so that everything could be set up in order, and that is why this relationship, which God had given to men, should also get its proper place. Thus, Christians must take this divinely given relationship up *in the Lord*. Among Christians, marriage must be *in the Lord*, and so it should be with every other relationship, too. For Christians, everything is *in the Lord*.

This applies primarily to marriage; the husband and his wife are one and should have only one will, i.e. they should always want the same things. No marriage can be happy if it is dominated by differing opinions. The husband must render her due to the wife. Many a marriage is spoiled, not because they do not love each other, but because they do not tell each other that they do! The Lord wants a husband to love his wife...

The Lord is very gracious with us and sympathises with our infirmities (Hebr. 4:15), but not with our sins. Sin has ruined everything, but because redemption has been accomplished at the cross we can turn back to the beginning, where everything is beautiful and lovely. If a marriage has not been contracted according to God's order, the children will not be able to take up their proper place towards their parents, and so forth. Even though *children* were given after the fall, they are nevertheless *sanctified on the basis of the death of Christ*; marriage, however, was instituted before the fall, and that is a beautiful figure of the Lord and the church or assembly. Marriage in the world becomes ever further removed from being a figure of this. We must not hold marriage in disregard; a Christian husband must not neglect his wife, nor the wife her husband.

Ezra 9:12 and 10:2; Nehemiah 13:23 and 24 give us an impression of how marriage to unbelievers was treated under the law, and 1 Cor. 7:12-17 shows us how it is under grace. The cover of Judaism was too short to cover the whole family (Ezra 10:19), but grace in the new covenant is sufficient for the whole family, so that the children are not unclean (1 Cor. 7:14). The children have their place, their angels continually behold the Father's face. The children are – *are far as the position is concerned* – holy. It is a question here of the Christian position. How all-encompassing Christianity is! It offers grace and room for all. Even the children are allowed to praise the Lord, for "out of the mouths of babes and sucklings thou has perfected praise."

Verse 29. "Brethren, the time is straitened. For the rest, that they who have wives, be as not having any." Think of Gideon's army (Judges 7). They did not first bow down on their knees, but lapped "with their hand to their mouth," so that their eyes could remain fixed on the leader. We are allowed to use earthly goods, but not to possess them, so that they do not hold sway over us. But what we possess and receive here on earth, is: God's mercy, compassion, goodness and favour.

The Lord connects us through *grace* with all that subsists in Christ beyond death.

Mercy is in connection with our relationships and our life on earth.

Peace keeps our hearts free and calm in the midst of trials, which are imposed on us here, and at the same time it allows us to enjoy His grace.

Thus, the Lord leaves it to His own whether or not to marry, but in any case, we should be free to serve *the Lord* (verse 35), and "wait on the Lord without distraction."

* * * * *

Preparation of Hearts for the Assembly

(Matthhew 14:22-33; 16:13-23)

In chapter 14, we see the preparation of a heart for Christian fellowship and in chapter 16 the manifestation of this condition.

The latter can be found neither in Mark, nor in Luke or John, although in John even the "brethren" are mentioned. In Matthew, the foundation pertaining to the assembly is laid and the collective side is considered. But first of all, we must be prepared for this; the individual side must be worked out in each one of us and the basis for this is salvation through His blood.

Chapter 14 teaches us that *Christianity* is *not a religion*, but is *centred in a Person*, whom we should follow. To get to know Him, we must first leave our own circumstances, just like Peter descended from the ship, to reach Him. In this passage, the ship represents our circumstances. The Lord knows our circumstances, His goodness and mercy follow us, but our circumstances imply the scene on this side of death, and therefore we cannot know Him in our own circumstances. But the assembly is associated with Him on the other side of death, in resurrection. There, He has brought us into association with Himself and His circumstances, so that we might prove His love. He is above all things, and *in Him* we are above all things. But Satan hates the Lord's testimony and he sets everything in motion to overthrow it, and so his attacks are especially directed towards the Christians who walk *in Him*.

Verse 23. The Lord goes up to a mountain apart to pray. ... While our circumstances develop down here, *the Lord exercises His priestly service for us.*

Verse 25. "In the fourth watch of the night" – in the darkest hour – He comes to them. He leaves His disciples with room, time and opportunity for heart exercise. He comes at the darkest moment. He never leaves His own to themselves. He is on high as our great High Priest, but at the same time He brings about spiritual heart exercises in us, and in the darkest hour He says: "it is I!" ... If the Lord alone is not enough for our pathway of faith, it is better not to tread it. It is a pathway on which the natural man cannot walk, he cannot even enter on it, he sinks. Many Christians discern *something* of the truth and the pathway of separation, keeping separate from other Christians etc., but it is all in vain if the Lord has not been reached on the other side of death, if His "it is I" is not enough for our pathway of faith, if we do not wait on the Lord alone. The waters here are a figure of the power of death. Christ walks upon the waters. He is above it, and we can be above it *in Him*, through *His power alone*, and *by His Spirit*. ... It is love that kindled a desire in Peter to be where He sees the Lord, and *love does not calculate*, it does not reconsider.

Many Christians find their satisfaction and rest in being Christian men and women, they want to join Christ to their own circumstances. But we should not be Christian *men* or *women*, but *Christians*. We must know Christ *beyond death*, we must stay away from human thoughts and not wish to connect our faith with what *we* are, but with Christ alone. But what is faith? Confidence in *Himself*. He is a *Person*, faith rests on a divine Person and not at all on us or on itself. By the Holy Scriptures we learn to believe, believe in a Person, *trust a Person*, namely the Lord alone. Therefore, nothing is more important than the Scriptures. – As long as a Christian has not reached Christ beyond death, he is confronted with the enemy's power against him; which is presented here in the strong wind.

But the Christian's position is with Christ on the waters. As the Lord entered into the ship, thus He also comes to His own in their circumstances and shows them goodness and mercy. But now, in the time of His absence, to reach Him and have part with Him, we must get to know Him beyond death, in resurrection. This applies to His assembly, and the truth connected with it is not earthly, but heavenly. He puts each one in specific circumstances here on earth, in different professions and positions in life, but if we want to know *Him* where He is, and *in connection with His assembly, we must seek Him beyond death.* This is the beginning. ... We are united to Him where He is.

The instruction in chapter 14 prepares the Christian for the truth of chapter 16.

Verse 13. "Who do men say that I the Son of man am?" etc. It is absolutely impossible for the natural man to know Christ, unless the Father reveals Him. His holy Person in the Godhead is always inscrutable for us, and it will always be so; it is only by the Father's revelation that we can know Him as the Son of man. "No one comes to the Son except the Father draw him."

In the same way, an unconverted person cannot comprehend the assembly, because he does not know Christ; it is utterly impossible to understand the assembly or church if you do not know Him, the Lord. And you can know much *about* Him without knowing Him.

Verse 15. "Who do ye say that I am?" The Lord's revelation given to Peter points at His resurrection. It means nothing but life. Everything there is life. By the death of Christ, all God's righteous requirements have been satisfied. The resurrection of Christ took place for us; it is for our justification.

The word Peter means 'stone'. "Petra" = a rock, as built on the truth; his relation to the Father was built on the revelation of the Son.

Verse 18. "Hades' gates." The gates of the cities were the place where counsel was held and judgment was executed. Thus, Satan and his authorities are holding counsel together, in order to destroy this new edifice, the Lord's assembly, the

Lord's stronghold on earth.

1 Timothy 1:16. The apostles served as examples for those about to believe on Him to life eternal.

In verse 19 (Matthew 16) it says: "the keys *of the kingdom of the heavens*," but not the keys of the assembly.

When we come together, we do so *in* assembly, but not as *the* assembly.

Verse 22. Peter's love for the Lord was greater than his faith. We can never trust our feelings; human feelings are not produced by the Holy Spirit.

We learn to understand the Lord not through His life, but through His death. It is only then that we can look back and admire how beautiful, how sublime His life was down here.

He has not yet "gone up into the ship." *He is still upon the waters* and it is there that we must reach Him. We want to draw near to Him, and reach Him as the Son of God. Death could not hold Him; every man is overcome by death, but He is the One who has overcome death. "He has the keys of death." "Be not afraid – *it is I*." Reaching Him beyond death does not mean any extraordinary feeling, but it is a real step; and once we have taken this step, it will bring us either persecution or temptation from the part of the enemy, but we can be confident, for He has said: "greater is he that is in you than he that is in the world."

Christ Continued in His Body on Earth

(Colossians 3:1-17)

Satan tries to get Christ out of the way. He definitely wanted to do away with Christ, as long as He walked on this earth, and now Christ is characterized and represented by His saints in His body here on earth. When He walked on earth, He always did the will of God, and now His will is to be carried out by His body. Christ is Head of the body. In Him we see the new man, in whom all nations are included (verse 11). They are a new creation in Christ, earthly names cease to be relevant; all believers form His body. This chapter contains exhortations (not doctrine; we find the doctrine in chapter 2) addressed to all those who represent the continuation of Christ in His body on earth. When the Holy Spirit came down, the continuation of Christ in His body commenced, and it has never ceased, but in Colossians we read nothing about the Holy Spirit, because it presupposes that His work in the saints has already been done; *Christ is at the centre of attention here and is continued in the saints.*

In the first chapter we find the Person of the Christ, in the second His doctrine, and in the third chapter the working out of His doctrine, the operation of the Christ in the saints.

Our life is not manifested in this world, it is hid in God (v. 3). The subject of this chapter is not so much eternal life, but the living operation of the Spirit in the saints.

The lives of the men of this world are not hidden; the greater their fame, the more their human life is made manifest; they have their reward! But the Christian's portion is still to come (v. 4). Their life is manifested in the holy city, presented figuratively in the gold and all the precious splendour. We walk in the city of the golden streets. We are separated from this world. As soon as we become faithful to the Lord, the world will no longer recognize us; our life belongs to a world to come. Christ asserts the position of greatest authority at the right hand of God. We are associated with Him, but the place at God's right hand shall never be the portion of the saints. Christ holds the sole title to this place. We are exhorted in this passage to manifest His mind, and our lives should answer to the Lord who has called us. We have not only been raised with the Christ (v. 1), but quickened together with Him (ch. 2:13), and when Christ returns, the Christians shall really be quickened in their bodies in Him. This is why in chapter 3:5 etc. we find exhortations. ... The assembly is not linked to the earth, it is a heavenly creation; but we, as the members of Christ, are on earth, and we are not allowed to give room to the old man, so that he cannot manifest his disposition. There are only two men: the old and the new man. The old man has been *put away by Christ*.

In Christ we see the new man, because He, His Person, is the second man out of heaven. As the new man, the Christians are associated with Him, ever fresh and beautiful to the eye of God, as trees planted by brooks of water. The epistle to the Colossians does not so much emphasize that we are a new creation in Christ, but in Him we are always fresh, as always drawing from Him and therefore remaining fresh and young. The features of Christ should characterize us and be continued in us: "renewed into full knowledge according to the image of him that has created him" (verse 10).

In the epistle to the Colossians, we find the Christian assembly; it is Christ, represented in the saints. In this epistle, the gospel is not presented to us, but His body, of which He alone is Head. In the verse "Walk in wisdom towards those without" etc. (ch. 4:5), it is not stated that we should live to Christ for the sake of the world, but a holy walk is presented as the consequence. We need wisdom towards those without, redeeming opportunities. In the present time, we gain knowledge, which should come to expression in our walk accordingly; in the world to come, this knowledge will give place to actuality, and it shall be manifested what we have known. – Verse 11: "Christ everything and in all," that is the new man, which we constitute with Him, who is our Head.

The epistle to the Colossians treats the saints *as a portrayal of Christ*, of His character, of His love (see verses 12 and 13). It is the best robe that we have to put on, it is the mind of Christ.

Verse 14. Love is a solid bond. It links everything together, like the links of a chain. It stands *over all*, it surpasses everything. *Christ did not have any character trait that stood out.* His character was perfectly even. He was the oblation of fine flour (Leviticus 2), which means everything in Him was perfect and perfectly balanced. Every man has a certain character and is strong in one respect, but weak in another, or, as we often say, he has his strengths and weaknesses. Man is always one-sided, he is never "at equilibrium." Christ was the only *perfect* Man. Well, love is the bond of perfectness.

Verse 15. "Let the peace of Christ preside in your hearts." We live in His tranquillity and in His rest. Christ was neither encouraged by a success, nor discouraged or weighed down by an apparent failure. He walked here in peace, the only perfect Man on earth. Peace shall reign in the world to come, but it should govern our hearts in one body already now.

Verse 15. "And be thankful." The world is not thankful. But *we should be characterized by thankfulness.*

Verse 16. "The word of the Christ" designates the whole *extent* of His doctrine, which he has brought to us. Everything is included in the expression "the word;" it does not say "the words," but "the word." – *Psalms* are the expression of our experiences, the expression of our hearts towards God about the way by which He has led us. *Hymns* are songs of praise and worship, addressed directly to divine Persons. *Spiritual songs* are about spiritual privileges and give praise for them. Singing is for God; it is the expression of the state of our hearts, when the heart is filled with worship and its desire is satisfied before God.

Verse 17. "Giving thanks to God" – what a beautiful image. Every thanksgiving gives joy and delight to God. It is for God's joy when we sing the praises with His Son (Hebrews 2:12-13).

Some Notes on Surrounding Countries
and more...

---oooOOOooo---

NOTES FROM POLAND

Concerning Bibles and New Testaments

I have been such a long time away from the country that my present activities are confined to a few individuals with whom I exchange correspondence, but I trust that the following may not be without interest. The other day I received a letter from the Secretary to the Governor of the Province in which I have lived in Poland. This secretary received one of the Bibles that you enabled me to purchase and evidently, he is being helped and no doubt not without exercise. He writes me that though the death of his mother he has been too full of grief to write, but assures me that he will he glad of our return to Poland.

A case not without interest occurred not long ago when a brother who had a Bible from you, was sent to prison for maintaining his position as a conscientious objector in bearing arms in accordance with the laws of conscription in force in Poland. When in prison, his Bible was taken from him, and blasphemy was written on its pages by the soldiers. He suffered not only from physical hunger and punishment, but also from the fact that he was denied the comfort of reading God's Word, having to rely upon his memory. Another soldier who witnessed these things was greatly impressed by the unjust conviction of this man, and having enquired my address he came to me, and after a talk, I, at his request gave him two copies of the New Testament, one for his own use, and the other for the comfort of the brother in prison. I afterwards learned that the New Testament was safely smuggled into the prison and was a means of comfort to the brother. The soldier later on came right out victorious as saved and is amongst us.

Another incident in connection with the distribution of the Bible amongst. enquirers occurs to me. An actress was converted in the meeting in Dubno and she began to confess Christ, of course giving up her profession to the anger and disgust of her husband, who turned against her at that time, and, because she could not obey him in respect of attendance at the theater, resulted in her being cast adrift in the streets. This sister in Christ bravely clung to the Truth and worked from farm to farm as an ordinary laborer and as such won the admiration of many who were once apposed to the Gospel. Her husband, seeing the wonderful testimony borne by his wife, repented of his action, and broken-heartedly appealed to his wife in return to him, promising that she would have absolute liberty concerning her faith. After being reconciled, her husband came to see me and begged a copy of the Scriptures. At first I wanted to give him simply a New Testament, but he would have a whole Bible; I found out that he was so greatly impressed by his wife's faith that he had determined to get hold of a whole Bible and to read it through in order to really test as to whether it was the Word of God or not. Naturally I recommended him to read firstly in the Gospels, but he refused and said, "If this book is the Word of God I will read from the beginning, as in that case the beginning must be as equally inspired as the New Testament." He commenced reading in this manner from Genesis and we were not a little concerned before our return to England to know that he was working through some of the Old Testament books with great difficulties. Prayer has been made for him for some time, and not long ago I was greatly cheered to receive a letter from Dubno to say that this man had reached the book of Ecclesiastes, and in reading that book had become so miserable and depressed that he was almost on the brink of suicide when he opened his heart to one of the local brethren who had the joy of pointing him to the Savior.

I have in Dubno something like 250 of such cases, and all of than have some such experience, which is honoring to the Word of God in testifying of the Lord Jesus Christ.

The brother Dubno who was formerly a Greek Catholic Priest and who has endured much persecution for the sake of the Lord Jesus Christ was saved through reading one of the Psalms. I cannot recall from memory which of the Psalms was used to his conversion, but converted he was, and immediately it meant for him a path of suffering as he was thrown out from home and lost everything belonging to this world.

Our united greetings and Christian love to Mrs. Lewis and yourself.

Yours very affectionately in the Lord Jesus Christ,

Fred. R. T. Adams

Concerning Poland

I have just received a letter from a Baptist brother, a White Russian, who I met in Brest- Litovsk in 1923.

Just before this, at the instigation of certain enemies of the truth, he had been ambushed and beaten severely by several men, so that he had been obliged to stay in bed for six weeks. Instead of using legal proceedings against the instigators of this assault, he showed a Christian spirit such that soon afterwards several of these men came to hear the preaching in a hotel where he lived.

I have been struck to see him so full of Christ, and we can surely pray for his spiritual blessing. We have provided him with literature for his personal reading, and tracts in White Russian and other languages for the population of this district.

F.W.Kingston

[ed.: A "White Russian" was name applied to Russians living in the countries between Russia and Poland.]

From a Brother in Poland

June 14, 1930

I thank you sincerely for all that you have done and that your heart is disposed to do more still. May the Lord recompense you according to His richest blessings. I can read German, although not very fluently. I have not had much opportunity to learn it. However, I would like to have some truly good and useful books. If the Lord puts this in your heart, I will be grateful for everything that you can send me. The tracts have been well received and everyone is very encouraged by them. I have asked the Lord that, by their means, He will present Himself to them as their Redeemer, Jesus Christ. Many remember you and your stay here in Poland. May the Lord bless you abundantly in His service, and may He encourage you to return to our country so that we can glorify the Lord together. I must ask you to forgive me for having taken so long to reply to your precious letter; I have been away.

With brotherly greetings

D

NORWAY and SWEDEN

TRANSLATION OF A LETTER TO J.H.L.

Dear Brother in the Lord,   Gothenburg, Sweden
August 11, 1928

We did not meet you in Norway, for wherever we came, you had been there just before us. It was a joy to me to accompany dear Gustafson. There was great interest in Tonsberg, and many came to the gospel, and the Lord spoke to souls. I hope the Lord's work there will prosper. It seemed hard in Horten, and no strangers came in to the gospel. There was great interest at Oslo, and many came out at each meeting. There was a nice feeling there. We had a good reading one evening on "the Kingdom" in the house of E. J. About 70 were present. We had 4 weeks, and visited all the meetings in Norway, except Ivedfjord. On our way home we had a very happy time at Halden. Dear Gustafson and his wife have now gone to Hallsberg far a few weeks. A. P. Erikson has been there, on his way home from the far north, where he visited the saints, much to their encouragement. Our brother Kollen motored several of us to Uddevalla, for a Lord's day, and two brothers from Halden, just over the Norwegian frontier, met us there. We had a very happy day, and the saints in Uddevalla were much cheered. Here in Gothenburg we are about as usual. Our meetings are well visited, and the Lord encourages us. With greetings from us all,

I remain, Your affectionate brother,

C. Sundberg

Translated from 'Quelques Nouvelles', inserted in the French magazine, 'Ondées'

From -- F.W.Kingston   March 1930

I am sure that you will be interested to learn that, through a meeting of a brother with a converted Bolshevik Russian, we have been put in touch with more than forty Christians who are working in Latvia, Lithuania, Estonia, and in other countries. For the most part, the men seem simple and devoted, probably having only a little light, but they are very desirous to spread the gospel. Thirty of them being able to read and appreciate ministry in the English language, we have sent them to begin with, a copy of the Outline of Genesis by CAC, with several books of FER and others, and we expect to continue sending them spiritual food, as the Lord may give us opportunity.

Then, according to the language of the population among whom these men are found, we have sent them tracts in Russian, Polish and German, as the case may be, to meet the needs of the population in their districts. This has also given us occasion to publish several tracts in the languages of these countries. Up to now, very little had been done in Lithuanian, Latvian, Estonian and Latgalian, and we are starting now to publish tracts in these languages. Eight tracts of CAC are translated into Latvian; at this point, they are being translated into Latgalian. If the Lord will, we will have in a few weeks 40,000 tracts in Latvian ready for distribution, and we hope that these will be followed by tracts in Latgalian and Estonian.

Until the Russian revolution, these little northern countries were part of the Russian empire; they are now separate independent countries. During the rule of the Russian czar, it was not possible either to print or circulate anything in the native languages of these little countries; the Russians allowed nothing. The door is now wide open, and one must give thanks for the fellowship of beloved saints, expressed not only in a practical way, but also in prayer.

"...the Word of God is not bound"

(A true story)

In the 1930s, Stalin, the Russian dictator, ordered massive purges of segments of the Soviet population to eliminate any whom he considered to be a threat to his rule. Christians (with their Bibles) were among the groups specially marked for elimination. Some historians estimate that over one million Christians died in Stalin's purges.

In Stavropol, Russia, Stalin's order to eliminate all Christians and all Bibles was strongly enforced. Thousands of Bibles were confiscated, while many Christians were immediately executed or sent to the gulags (prisons) where most died, branded as "enemies of the state."

Many years later, when Soviet persecution of Christians had greatly eased, a Christian missionary team, was allowed to visit Stavropol to make contact with any Christians living there. However, the Bibles they had ordered from Moscow to distribute in Stavropol had not arrived. A local Russian who knew the history of the Stavropol purges mentioned that the warehouse where the confiscated Bibles had been stored still existed.

A member of the missionary team went to the warehouse to see if the Bibles were still there. The warehouse officials assured him that they were indeed still stored there. A request to remove the Bibles and to distribute them to the people of Stavropol also received official approval.

The next day the missionary team returned with a truck and with several Russian men who had been hired to help load the Bibles. One of these, a young college student, was particularly hostile and arrogant, a self-proclaimed agnostic. It was obvious he had come just to earn a day's wages.

While loading the Bibles one of the missionaries noticed that the young man had disappeared. When they found him, he was huddled in the corner of the warehouse holding a Bible in his hands and weeping. He had planned to take one of the Bibles for himself and had stolen away from the truck unnoticed so that none would know that he too wanted a Bible.

Once alone with a pile of Bibles, he had picked up a dusty, well-worn copy. Opening it, he was deeply shaken when he saw, inside the front cover, the faded hand-writing and name of the Bible's former owner – one of the Christians who had been purged by Stalin so many years before – his own grandmother.

So shall My word be that goeth forth out of My mouth: it shall not return unto Me void, but it shall accomplish that which I please, and it shall prosper in the thing whereto I sent it. Isaiah 55:11

www.ingramcontent.com/pod-product-compliance
Lightning Source LLC
Chambersburg PA
CBHW071304040426
42444CB00009B/1863